Odds'R™

The Odds On EVERYTHING BOOK™

Roger L. Schlaifer

THE ODDS ON EVERYTHING BOOK™

A Bantam Book / November 2005

Published by Bantam Dell
A Division of Random House, Inc.
New York, New York

And introducing Oddsworth,™ our Wizard of Odds **Do Tell!**

Copyright © 2005 by Roger L. Schlaifer
All rights reserved

Book and Cover Design by Tim Dove

Bantam Books and the rooster colophon are
registered trademarks of Random House, Inc.

Odds'R and The Odds On Everything Book are trademarks of
Schlaifer Nance & Company, Inc., and the Odds'R Network, Inc.

Library of Congress Cataloging-in-Publication Data
is on file with the publisher.

ISBN-13: 978-0-553-38346-1
ISBN-10: 0-553-38346-9

Printed in the United States of America
Published simultaneously in Canada

www.bantamdell.com

BVG 10 9 8 7 6 5 4 3 2 1

WARNING!

You may be shocked or offended by some of the contents of *Odds'R—The Odds On Everything Book*. For the former, it's a good reason to read the book, and for the latter, it's a better reason to reconsider your therapist or think about going twice a week.

<u>Do not depend solely on this book in making any major, or even relatively minor, life decisions</u>. If we've learned nothing else in researching this book it's that every situation is subject to lots of variables. Furthermore, due to ADD staffers and questionable work habits there is a possibility—or, as a statistician might put it, *a reasonable probability within an acceptable standard deviation*, that mistakes have been made. Not just by our stellar group of fact finders and proofreaders, whose scrutiny precludes most human error, but because we rely on external data gathering sources like polling organizations, news articles, and (shudder) the U.S. government—which often updates and corrects data only sporadically.

The statistics we present are the most reliable and up-to-date at the time of our research. Note that we've often rounded off the odds and percentages, since actuarial accuracy isn't what this book is about. Pedants and probalists requiring more sophisticated mathematical maneuverings should read books by Dr. Robert Hogg, Pasqual Beyes, and Robert O. Schlaifer (yes, a second cousin). But for most of us, these tomes are, like, *seriously* dense.

We welcome input and *kind* commentary on odds, oddities, and this current Q&A collection. If you have ideas for making anything funnier or more surprising, send them in—but don't expect any remuneration. Our charitable pledges have already been made.

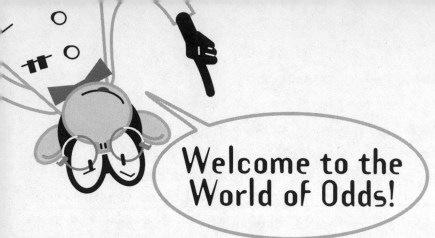

Welcome to the World of Odds!

Why Odds?

Facts and statistics, by themselves, are pretty useless. Because they require interpretation, they're coveted material for lawyers, politicians, and the media in whose hands they often spin from straw to gold.

Odds give you an edge in deciding what to do next—whether it's something prescribed by your physician, recommended by your stockbroker, or suggested by a hot date. An alternative to the bunker or revolution—with a few laughs in the process, some courtesy of our resident oddsmaker, Oddsworth, pictured above.

We, of course, have our own perspective on the stats and facts we've gathered. The goal in assembling them here is to provide you with information in a practical and entertaining format—one that presents statistics in edible (even tasty) portions—especially when taken with a grain of salt.

What Do the Odds Mean?

Odds are the mathematical projections that particular events will or won't occur and are usually expressed as a ratio of those possibilities. So, if the odds of a plane crash are 1 to 1 million (or, alternatively, 1 in 1 million), then the chance of there being a plane crash is extremely low. That might sound counterintuitive—largely because of our familiarity with gambling odds (more below)—but that's the correct mathematical expression.

On the other hand, when your odds of dying from the bite of a Black Mamba are 99 to 1, (or alternatively, a 99 in 100 chance) wear the heavy leather boots and watch where you're walking! Better yet, stay out of the jungle.

As you've seen, chance is another way of expressing odds or probabilities. For instance, a 1 in 500 chance is a pretty low probability that what you were hoping for, or were afraid of, would occur. And for clarity we have often used chance instead of odds in framing the questions in this book. After all, we didn't want to trip you up—at least not on semantics.

When there's a certainty that something won't happen, it's expressed as "zero" probability. If there's a 50% or 50-50 chance, it's called "even odds," sometimes expressed as 1 to 1. At the opposite end of the probability spectrum are absolute certainties of occurrence. These are expressed as "100%"—since there's no chance they won't occur. And that's somewhat rare, much like the chance of not seeing another double negative in this book.

The odds (and probabilities) in this book are generally based on the real possibility that something may or may not happen, calculated on the population engaged in the particular activity or event and on other conditional factors. But this is an entertaining presentation (we hope!) not an academic one. And we have often used "most likely, least likely," and the colloquial "odds are" instead of numerical expressions to convey the odds.

Finally, don't make the mistake of confusing the odds in this book with the "book" you get from your bookie. Those ratios, while expressed as "odds," are really just the ratios of the payout for each dollar bet. For more on that, check out our game.*

GOT IT?

*For more on *Odds'R®—The Odds On Everything Game*, visit our website at: **www.oddsrgames.com**.

CONTENTS

In Memory of Dad—

For inspiring me with his generosity,
good humor, and endless curiosity.

Test Yourself!

Sure, you can just read *Odds'R®—The Odds On Everything Book*. You can even read it aloud on the subway/train/bus/taxi on your way to work/school/rehab/court/colonoscopy.

But if you're not taking it as a test, you're missing half the fun. There's no proctor, no postevaluation to send you running back to analysis, and no need to drink heavily after the examination. Drink *during* the exam.

Oh, and be sure to keep score as you go along. Even if your score sucks, you can memorize the answers and bet your unwitting friends. After all, it's *your* book.

Good Luck!

Forward!

Life
or
Death

❝It's not that I'm afraid of dying,
I just don't want to be there when it happens!**❞**
— WOODY ALLEN —

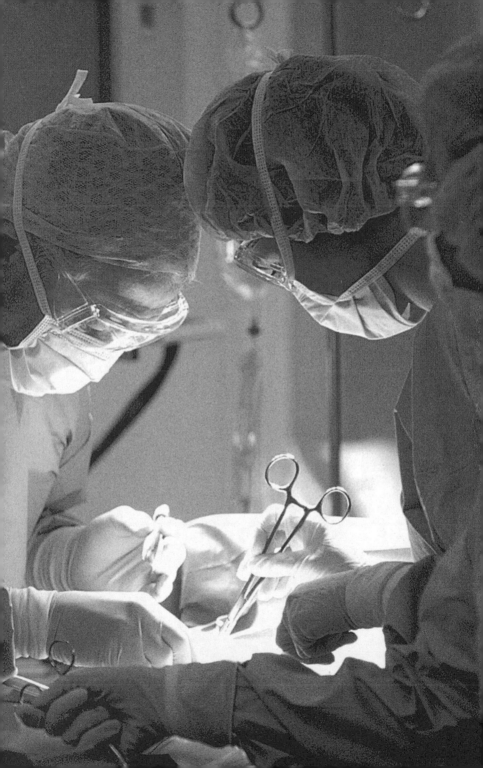

What are your odds of surviving a barrel ride over Niagara or a routine surgical procedure? Are you more likely to survive a run-in with a deer or the running of the bulls in Pamplona? Will your suicidal friend leave a note?

Whether you're 18 or 80 we've got the numbers—and the odds of living or dying in predicaments from the mundane to the monstrous.

Scalpel, Forceps...
1 ## Embalming Fluid—
You're most likely to die from which of the following surgeries?

A) Liposuction
B) Hernia
C) Hip Replacement

ANSWER ▶

Buried Assets—
2 You'll most likely pay which of the following for the average funeral in the U.S.?

A) $6,500
B) $9,500
C) $12,500

ANSWER ▶

Bagged by Your Dry Cleaner—
3 Your lifetime chance of being suffocated by a plastic laundry bag is which of the following?

A) 1 in 3,000
B) 1 in 13,000
C) 1 in 130,000

ANSWER ▶

1 C) Hip Replacement

Of the 120,000 hip replacements performed annually, about 400 patients die from complications within three months of the surgery—most often because of the advanced age of the patient. Liposuction sucks the fat—and the life—out of about 80 people annually. And hernia surgery, though a pain in the groin, is responsible for only an estimated 40 deaths out of the 800,000 procedures done annually.

Source: CDC 2004

◀ QUESTION

2 A) $6,500

You can't take it with you, so leave a healthy chunk close at hand. The average funeral costs about $6,500. Switch from a wood casket to copper and you're up to $10K; bronze runs twice as much. And for those who insist on having the last laugh, a German company now manufactures "wacky coffins" shaped like everything from Mercedeses and tuxedos to—onions!

Source: NFDA 2004

◀ QUESTION

3 C) 1 in 130,000

There's no reason to end up with a tag on your toe instead of your top, but each year 27 people turn up as stiff as their own starched shirts by not taking those clingy clothes wraps seriously enough. Turns out mob money isn't the only thing it's dangerous to launder.

Source: CDC 2004

◀ QUESTION

Bull Run—

4

Over the 80 years of the "running of the bulls" in Pamplona, Spain, what are the chances that a runner, once run over, *didn't* live to tell the tale?

A) 7 in 100
B) 35 in 100
C) 75 in 100

ANSWER ▶

Snow Exit—

5

Between 1989 and 2004, in which state was it likeliest that someone would die in an avalanche?

The Ultimate Whine Cooler!

A) Alaska
B) Colorado
C) Idaho

ANSWER ▶

Just Chillin'—

6

What's your lifetime chance of dying from suffocation in a refrigerator or some other "airtight" space?

A) 1 in 27,000
B) 1 in 270,000
C) 1 in 2,700,000

ANSWER ▶

4 **A) 7 in 100**

Since Hemingway first glamorized this questionable tradition in *The Sun Also Rises,* more than 200 people have been injured in the running of the bulls. Of those, only 14 have died. Of course, if the unsuspecting bulls realized that their day would likely end by being stabbed, castrated, and de-eared as a matador's prize, we suspect that the casualties would be much higher.

Source: National Geographic; *CNN 2004*

◀ Q U E S T I O N

5 **B) Colorado**

It's a Rocky Mountain low for the 90 hapless souls buried in Colorado avalanches. Alaska ranks a grim second with 73. Only 21 have perished in Idaho avalanches, and we suspect that some of those may have gone down in a flood of mashed potatoes.

Source: geosurvey.state.co.us/avalanche, U.S. World Stats 2004

◀ Q U E S T I O N

6 **B) 1 in 270,000**

Keeping freshness in means keeping oxygen out. Thirteen people a year—usually kids—still die in this very uncool fashion—far fewer than in the 1950s when stringent safety regulations were passed. *(And no—we've been unable to find any reports of someone dying inside a working refrigerator. Probably because the door is opened about a hundred times a day.)*

Source: NSC 2003

◀ Q U E S T I O N

7

"Hey, Guys? We're Out of Peanuts!"

When the Uruguay rugby team crashed into the Andes in 1972, what was the chance of a survivor of the ordeal staying alive by eating the flesh of other, *dead* passengers?

A) 25%
B) 50%
C) 100%

ANSWER ▶

8

Power Surge!

Which of the following home appliances is most likely to get someone electrocuted?

Shocking Results!

A) Air Conditioner
B) Hair Dryer
C) Electric Drill

ANSWER ▶

9

Look! Up in the Sky! It's...OW!

What is your lifetime chance of being killed by a falling object?

A) 1 in 4,900
B) 1 in 49,000
C) 1 in 490,000

ANSWER ▶

7   C) 100%

Spending 71 days lost and without food in the snow-covered Andes made the unthinkable thinkable, and, ultimately, do-able—as the 16 rugby players who survived clearly showed. But none of the agony they went through prepared them for the really brutal ordeal of having to watch Ethan Hawke and Vince Spano play them in the movie.

Source: Alive, Piers Paul Read

◀ QUESTION

8   A) Air Conditioner

We don't exactly know how, but according to government reports, the air conditioner is responsible for 14 electrocution deaths annually—more than the hair dryer and electric drill *combined*. Just when you thought it was safe to take your Carrier 52F into the bathtub...

Source: CPSC 2004

◀ QUESTION

9   A) 1 in 4,900

When someone dies suddenly, it may seem to come "out of thin air," but a particularly unlucky group experiences that sensation a bit more literally. In fact, just over 700 people are struck and killed by falling objects each year. *(Those struck by falling apples are more likely to survive— and have scientific epiphanies!)*

Source: NSC 2004

◀ QUESTION

Fumes-Day Scenario—

10

What is your lifetime chance of *accidentally* dying in a car from motor vehicle exhaust?

A) 1 in 7,000
B) 1 in 11,000
C) 1 in 19,000

A N S W E R ▶

Golden Gate Toll—

11

Since San Francisco's Golden Gate opened in 1937, there have been 1,300 suicide attempts from the bridge, giving 2 in 5 odds that a future attempt will likely result in which of the following?

A) Death
B) Being Stopped
C) Surviving the Leap

A N S W E R ▶

Crush Hour—

12

When you get that "put-upon" feeling from a heavy piece of machinery, what is your lifetime chance that you'll be breathing your last breath?

A) 1 in 5,700
B) 1 in 57,000
C) 1 in 570,000

A N S W E R ▶

10 **C) 1 in 19,000**

About 190 people a year get gassed accidentally in their own cars. And that number doesn't even count the ill effects of those dangling air "fresheners." The moral here would seem to be: *Don't leave your engine running—even for a chance to get lucky in the backseat.*

Source: NSC 2004

◀ QUESTION

11 **B) Being Stopped**

A 4-foot railing and human intervention are the only deterrents to suicide on the Golden Gate. But police or bystanders have thwarted 515 suicidal souls, only 1 of whom is known to have made a later, successful attempt from the bridge. Of those who have taken the 200-foot, 75-mph plunge, 98% have died.

Source: USA Today 2005

◀ QUESTION

12 **A) 1 in 5,700**

"Don't look now!" are not the words you want to hear as the hair on your neck jolts to red alert. Maybe those *Matrix* guys aren't so paranoid after all. In addition to causing thousands of occupational injuries, machines permanently flatten around 1,100 people annually. *(Surely that can't be kosher with OSHA.)*

Source: NSC 2002

◀ QUESTION

A Real Sinking Feeling—

13 What's your lifetime chance of drowning?

A) 1 in 900
B) 1 in 9,000
C) 1 in 90,000

ANSWER ▶

Squish! You Were Here—

14 Being caught between bases can be a sure "Out!" in baseball. What is the chance of having the life squeezed out of you by being caught between hard "objects"?

A) 1 in 320
B) 1 in 3,200
C) 1 in 32,000

ANSWER ▶

Vaporized—

15 What is your chance of being done in this year by poisonous gas or vapor (other than carbon monoxide)?

A) 1 in 435,000
B) 1 in 43,500
C) 1 in 4,350

ANSWER ▶

13 **A) 1 in 900**

Better hang on to those floaties! About 3,300 people a year end up in Davy Jones's locker. *(And no, we don't mean the one from the Monkees.)* The "final ablution" is a mix of about 600 in pools, 1,000 in natural bodies of water, and about 300 in bathtubs; the others are lumped into an "unspecified" category of drownings. Wells? Pails? Toilet bowls? *(We don't know; use your imagination.)*

Source: NSC 2003

◄ QUESTION

14 **C) 1 in 32,000**

Each year about 118 folks are actually crushed to death— often between the aptly named "pinch rollers" used on chain drives, feed rollers, and—OUCH!— gear drives, giving a whole new meaning to the word *flatliners*.

Source: NSC 2003

◄ QUESTION

15 **A) 1 in 435,000**

The odds are pretty good that you won't be one of the 550 people to die this year of poison gas or vapor. And your *lifetime* chance of being "vaporized" is only 1 in 6,000, so you can shove that gas mask back in your Homeland Security Safety Kit.

Source: NSC 2004

◄ QUESTION

Hard to Swallow?

16 Your lifetime chance of dying is about 1 in 5,000 from which of the following?

A) Food Poisoning
B) Object in Throat
C) Food in Throat

ANSWER ▶

Ciao via Plow—

17 Your lifetime chance of being killed by a bulldozer, earthmover, or other excavating equipment is:

Can You Dig It?

A) 1 in 4,500
B) 1 in 45,000
C) 1 in 450,000

ANSWER ▶

Barreled Over—

18 If you were one of the daredevils who tried to barrel over Niagara Falls between 1901 and 2004, what were your chances of surviving the ride?

A) 30%
B) 50%
C) 80%

ANSWER ▶

16 B) Object in Throat

Chew first, then swallow! While this advice might lose you your job if you were Linda Lovelace (may she R.I.P.), it would save a lot of lives. Nonedible, hard objects lodged in throats kill over 3,000 people annually, more than 4 times the 742 deaths from choking and inhaling food. As for accidentally being poisoned to death by a lethal comestible, your chance of dying is about one in a million—even in Ukraine.

Source: CDC 2004

◀ Q U E S T I O N

17 B) 1 in 45,000

Who knew CATs and Deeres could be so dangerous? The serious downside of buildings going up is that around 80 people a year go under from unfortunate encounters with earthmovers. On the upside, it could save your family a bundle on burial costs.

Source: NSC 2004

◀ Q U E S T I O N

18 C) 80%

Wow! Despite dropping 75 feet in less than 3 seconds, 4 out of 5 plungers have lived to boast about it. Among the survivors was the first person "man enough" to attempt the feat—63-year-old Annie Taylor—in 1901. Excluding David Copperfield's 1990 Niagara stunt (after all, he is a magician), there have been 15 attempts involving 17 people—including two sets of couples and one guy without a barrel!

Source: Niagara Parks Commission 2004

◀ Q U E S T I O N

Butting Out—

19 Which of the following digestive disorders is *least* likely to kill you?

A) Constipation
B) Hemorrhoids
C) Diarrhea

ANSWER ▶

Slip Slidin' Away—

20 What is your chance of being buried alive in a landslide?

Make Mine a Kahlúa & Cream!

A) 1 in 6,400
B) 1 in 64,000
C) 1 in 640,000

ANSWER ▶

A Current Affair—

21 We all know that we're composed of 90% water, right? And water does what? Yep, it conducts electricity. As one of those ordinary vessels of water, what is your chance of being electrocuted at home or on the job?

A) 1 in 6,000
B) 1 in 60,000
C) 1 in 600,000

ANSWER ▶

19   ## B) Hemorrhoids

Pile on all the disgusting jokes you want, apparently almost nobody (well, only 16) dies from hemorrhoids and the embarrassment they might cause. That number nearly doubles to 28 for the 3 million constipation sufferers in the U.S., while infectious diarrhea drains almost 3,100 a year, a stat that's truly Pepto-*Dismal!*

Source: NDDIC; NIH 2004

◀ Q U E S T I O N

20   ## C) 1 in 640,000

Not bad odds, but each year, between 25 and 55 Americans are buried without benediction, casket, or even the customary courtesy of being certified dead first. Landslides in the U.S. occur mostly in California, though Utah, Alaska, Hawaii, and Washington have had some of the worst in U.S. history.

Source: NSC 2003

◀ Q U E S T I O N

21   ## A) 1 in 6,000

The shocking news is that on average, over 400 Americans take an annual one-way electric slide into the beyond. That doesn't include electric chair casualties (still legal in ten states), bolts out of the blue (40 to 50 deaths annually), or the unlucky 150 who are severely singed at gas pumps from the buildup of static electricity (often from cell phones) suddenly igniting the fuel.

Source: NSC 2004

◀ Q U E S T I O N

Living Large—

22

If you're obese it is most likely that you will eventually end up in which of the following?

A) Oversized Ambulance
B) Supersized Casket
C) Funeral at Age 46

ANSWER ▶

From Doe to DOA—

23

"Caught in the headlights!" has an entirely different meaning when the car you're driving collides with a deer. What is the chance of such a collision turning deadly for the driver?

A) 1 in 100
B) 1 in 1000
C) 1 in 10,000

ANSWER ▶

Taking a Dive—

24

What are the chances that a dive you take (into a body of water, not "in the ring") will be your last?

A) 1 in 3,100
B) 1 in 31,000
C) 1 in 310,000

ANSWER ▶

22   ## C) Funeral at Age 46

Live fat, die young. Obese people are 6 times more likely to develop heart disease and *10 times* more likely to develop diabetes and kidney failure than their normal-sized neighbors, giving them far fewer years than the U.S. average of 77.6. As for a ride on a retrofitted, large-body ambulance or being carted off to the cemetery in a supersized casket, their use is still limited, but expanding to meet demand.

Source: NIH; Am. Ambulance Assoc.; Am. Obesity Assoc. 2004

◀ Q U E S T I O N

23   ## C) 1 in 10,000

Back off, Bambi! Between the explosion in the deer population and growing traffic in outlying areas, there are over 520,000 deer-related accidents a year, resulting in the deaths of over 50 drivers—and lots of deer.

Source: Insurance Information Institute 2004

◀ Q U E S T I O N

24   ## C) 1 in 310,000

Going headlong into anything—even water—can wreak havoc with your head, especially when the water's not as deep as you thought (less than 10 feet deep) or is hiding objects harder than your head. The yearly toll of DOA or catastrophically injured divers in the U.S. is between 800 and 900—mostly male, often drunk. (Duh!)

Source: NSCIC; Dr. Tom Griffiths 2005

◀ Q U E S T I O N

Take Two and Call Me in the <u>Mourning</u>—

25

Your odds of accidentally escaping the stress of daily life—permanently—are about 2.5 million to 1 with which of the following *legal* drugs?

A) Barbiturates
B) Nonbarbiturate Sedatives
C) Tranquilizers

ANSWER ▶

Postcards from the Ledge—

26

What's the chance of a suicide victim leaving a note?

Say It with Flowers!

A) 1 in 6
B) 1 in 8
C) 1 in 10

ANSWER ▶

Gag Me with a Spoon—

27

What are the odds that a girl who is anorexic will become bulimic when she goes off to college?

A) 1 to 1
B) 1 to 4
C) 1 to 8

ANSWER ▶

25   C) Tranquilizers

Even with tranquilizers—the most lethal of the bunch—a journey through the Valley of the Dolls doesn't often lead to the Valley of Death. Only about 100 accidental deaths in the U.S. each year result from the use of tranquilizers. Another 16 result from the use of barbiturates and 8 from other sedatives and hypnotics. So you can stay calm as you count out your Yellow Jackets, Blue Devils, and Red Birds.

Source: NSC 2004

◀ Q U E S T I O N

26   A) 1 in 6

Trash the guilt. With less than 20% of victims leaving a note, you'll probably never know exactly what made them do it. *(Although the 63 new voicemail messages from collection agencies could be a clue.)*

Source: FriendsforSurvival.org

◀ Q U E S T I O N

27   A) 1 to 1

It's enough to make you want to throw up! Half the anorexics who begin by starving themselves end up deliberately purging. And it's deadly for about 20% of sufferers, including singer Karen Carpenter who died in 1983 from a heart attack caused by her years of bulimia, and gymnast Christy Henrich who died in 1994 from complications of anorexia at age 22, weighing only 47 lbs.!

Source: PDRHealth.com; UVanderbilt

◀ Q U E S T I O N

From "F.U." to R.I.P.—

28 What's the chance that a road-rage incident will end in someone's death?

A) 1 in 350
B) 1 in 1,100
C) 1 in 2,700

ANSWER ▶

Drills, Spills, or Overfills—

29 Which of the following is most likely to be deadly?

I'll Take the Least Likely to Succeed!

A) Using Power Tools
B) Falling Off a Roof
C) Being Caught in a Cave-In

ANSWER ▶

Hot Topic—

30 Your odds of dying in a fatal house fire are greatest if you or someone you're with is:

A) Cooking
B) Smoking
C) In Debt to the Mob

ANSWER ▶

28 B) I in 1,100

Think twice before flashing the bird to that idiot trying to pass you on the right. It's not going to change your life—unless you let it escalate into one of the more than 200 deaths and 12,600 injuries attributed to road rage in the U.S. since 1990. Why mix it up with a perfect stranger when you can go home and take it out on your family, your dog, or your neighbor?

Source: AAA 2004

◀ Q U E S T I O N

29 B) Falling Off a Roof

Maybe these guys were (mostly) sleeping in school the day they taught us about GRAVITY, because over 143 die each year from falling off rooftops—more than from cave-ins (116) and power tool use (7) combined. *(Let's go over this again: the thing about gravity is that if you're up really high...)*

Source: NCFOI 1996

◀ Q U E S T I O N

30 A) Cooking

You're more likely to be done in by the cook than the Marlboro man. Social smokers who "only smoke when they're drinking" increase the risk of fire by 60%. As for arson, the Mob employs it only in cases of business liquidation, not debt repayment. That's usually handled with a Louisville Slugger.

Source: NSC 2004

◀ Q U E S T I O N

Blights Out—

31 If you were living in Ireland during the potato famine of 1846–50, what was your chance of dying from starvation or disease attributable to the famine?

A) 1 in 10
B) 1 in 4
C) 1 in 20

ANSWER ▶

Fin de Schwinn—

32 What are the odds of the victim of a fatal bicycle accident being male rather than female?

Pedal to the Metal!

A) 2 to 1
B) 4 to 1
C) 7 to 1

ANSWER ▶

The Hills Are Alive...

33 What is your chance, in any given year, of dying from the bite of a fire ant?

A) 1 in 50,000
B) 1 in 500,000
C) 1 in 5,000,000

ANSWER ▶

31   **B) 1 in 4**

Approximately 1.7 million people in Ireland died during the potato famine. Of those, almost half died aboard "coffin" ships as they tried to emigrate to the U.S. and other countries. By the beginning of 1851 Ireland's population had dropped from 8 million to about 5 million.

Source: USEPA/History

◀ Q U E S T I O N

32   **C) 7 to 1**

Dudes may think they look cool weaving through traffic and speeding along dangerous biking trails, but when it comes to finishing the ride alive, guys are 8 times more likely to end up dead than their—*did someone say smarter?*—female counterparts.

Source: NIIHS 2004

◀ Q U E S T I O N

33   **C) 1 in 5,000,000**

The bad news: over *5 million* Americans are stung by fire ants every year. The good news: an average of only 1 fatality per year. The other bad news is that these tiny terrors latch onto your skin with barbed mandibles and stab you repeatedly with spiked tails, creating burning pustules that can last for 10 days. The other *good* news is, well…there really is no other good news about fire ants.

Source: UTexas/Austin/Gilbert; safe2use.com

◀ Q U E S T I O N

Wait! Who Ordered the Stake?

34 If you had been arrested for witchcraft during the infamous Salem witch hunt and trials of 1692, what would have been your chance of being executed?

A) 1 in 4
B) 1 in 8
C) Zero (brooms, y'know)

ANSWER ▶

The Rockets' Dead Glare—

35 Odds are, in your average year, which number of Americans will be killed by fireworks?

Let's Fire One Up!

A) 1
B) 6
C) 21

ANSWER ▶

The Hippocratic Oaf—

36 What is your chance of dying from a medical complication due to a surgical mistake (a "misadventure," as it's called in the trade) or other medical care?

A) 1 in 1,100
B) 1 in 5,500
C) 1 in 11,000

ANSWER ▶

34 **B) 1 in 8**

Over 150 people were arrested for witchcraft during this period of mass hysteria. Of those, 20 were executed, 3 died in prison, and one 80-year-old man—in a turn that would make the Wicked Witch of the West proud—was "pressed to death" by heavy stones. There were 2 reports of escapes—whether as bats or cats is not known—and 2 dogs were executed, *just in case.*

Source: salemwitchcrafttrials.com 2004

◄ Q U E S T I O N

35 **B) 6**

There were 84 fireworks-related deaths between 1988 and 2001, an average of 6 victims a year. Not surprisingly, most of them occurred during the month of July—though a few blasted their way into their last New Year. Serious injuries from fireworks—almost all in nonprofessional uses—totaled 9,300 in 2004.

Source: CPSC 2004

◄ Q U E S T I O N

36 **A) 1 in 1,100**

No wonder they call it "practicing" medicine. Nobody's perfect, but with an estimated 44,000 to 98,000 deaths a year attributable to medical errors, it behooves us all to do a little more than "kick the tires" when we're looking for medical care. *(And if your doctor is named Kevorkian, you might want to get a second opinion.)*

Source: NSC 2004

◄ Q U E S T I O N

Hardhead Area—

37 What are the chances that a person killed riding a bicycle was *not* wearing a helmet?

A) 20%
B) 55%
C) 85%

ANSWER ▶

Loose Ends—

38 You are most likely to contract deadly diarrhea from which of the following?

No Ifs, Ands, or Butts!

A) Hospital/Nursing Home
B) Public Drinking Water
C) A Beef Burrito

ANSWER ▶

A Well-Urned Rest—

39 If you're residing in the U.S. when you die, what are the chances that you'll be cremated?

A) 18%
B) 28%
C) 48%

ANSWER ▶

37 ## C) 85%

We're not saying they died because they weren't wearing a helmet, we're just pointing out that 85% of bicycle fatalities were helmetless. And if you can read that stat and still ride your bike without a helmet, there's probably not that much in your head worth protecting.

Source: NIIHS 2004

◀ *Q U E S T I O N*

38 ## A) Hospital/Nursing Home

Unless you're sucking on the spout, public drinking fountains are pretty safe, as are bites from most burritos. But in hospitals and nursing homes, the *C. difficile* bacterium appears to be running rampant—infecting over 3 million people in the U.S. each year, of which about 3,000 die. This is particularly problematic for the elderly, who have trouble running anywhere—even to the bathroom.

Source: CDC; AHRP 2004

◀ *Q U E S T I O N*

39 ## B) 28%

Over a quarter of those who die in the U.S. each year end up powdering their noses—and everything else. But not every state is burning at the same rate. Nevada leads the nation in cremation, with 65%. Alabama is at the low end of the scale, burning only 4.5%—*not counting crosses.*

Source: NFDA 2004

◀ *Q U E S T I O N*

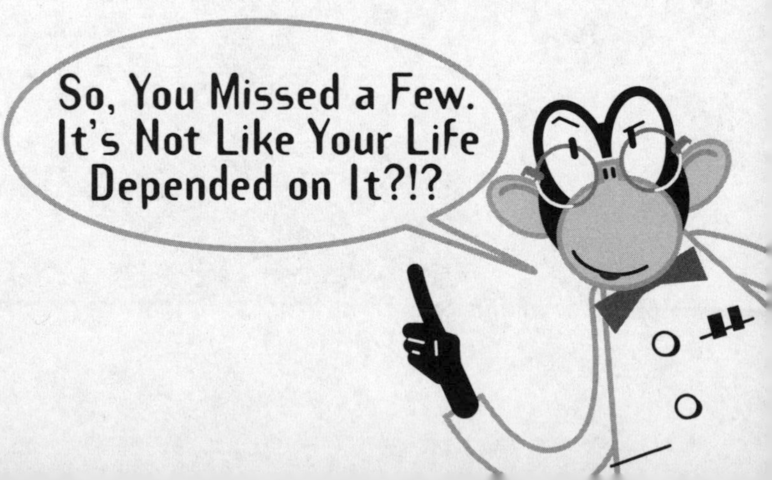
So, You Missed a Few.
It's Not Like Your Life
Depended on It?!?

2

Health
&
Happiness

66 Happiness is good health—and a bad memory. 99
— INGRID BERGMAN —

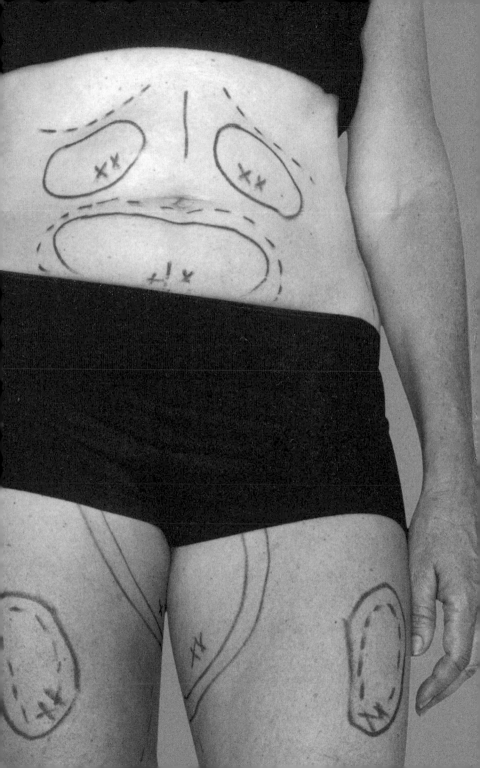

What's the chance of living to 100? Will plastic surgery build you up, smooth you out, or take you down? How likely are you to "catch something" in the hospital? Do most Americans support your position on medical marijuana (or are they too stoned to care)?

Fit or fat, you're about to face the facts of health and happiness.

A Simple Twist of Fat—

1 While 85% of dieters lose weight on their diets, what are the chances of their keeping it off for 2 years or more?

A) 55%
B) 24%
C) 15%

ANSWER ▶

Undercover Activity—

2 Other than sleeping, the chance is 1 in 5 that you'll be doing which of the following in bed tonight?

A) Smoking
B) Snoring
C) Having Sex

ANSWER ▶

Internal Repairs—

3 The first U.S. human organ transplant was performed on December 23, 1954, in Boston. For which of the following organs is an American most likely to be seeking a transplant today?

A) Intestine
B) Kidney
C) Liver

ANSWER ▶

1 **C) 15%**

No pain when you gain—and you can go back to wearing those large sizes you were smart enough to keep in your closet. Then, of course, the guilt kicks in, and you start dieting again. It's kind of a Fats Domino effect.

Source: MediResource.com 2004

◀ Q U E S T I O N

2 **B) Snoring**

While fewer folks puff on the pillows these days, it's estimated that 20% of adults snore at night. Since the typical snorer is overweight, has high blood pressure, and has consumed alcohol shortly before bedtime, is it any wonder that the chance of the average adult having sex—*with someone else*—is less than 1 in 6?

Source: CDC; NCHS 2004

◀ Q U E S T I O N

3 **B) Kidney**

Of the more than 86,000 Americans currently waiting for organ transplants, the large majority—almost 59,000—are in need of a kidney. Livers are the second-most-needed organ, while only a couple of hundred people are waiting for intestines...*discounting fans of haggis and menudo, of course.*

Source: UNOS, Organ Donor Program 2004

◀ Q U E S T I O N

All-Consuming—

4 In the U.S., you are most likely to die from a food-borne pest caused by which of the following?

A) Bacteria
B) Parasite
C) Virus

ANSWER ▶

No, You Can't Cut'em Open to Count Their Rings!

5 What is the chance an American is 100 years old or older?

A Wrinkle in Time!

A) 1 in 5,000
B) 1 in 50,000
C) 1 in 500,000

ANSWER ▶

Chest Intentions—

6 What are the odds that a woman who had her breast implants removed would have them replaced within a year?

A) Even odds
B) 2 to 1
C) 4 to 1

ANSWER ▶

4   ## A) Bacteria

Viruses may be the stock-in-trade of thriller novels, and parasites really suck, but bacteria are responsible for over 70% of America's food-borne fatalities. In fact, just 2 of the minute beasties alone—nontyphoidal salmonella (30.6%) and *Listeria monocytogenes* (27.6%)—cause the majority of these deaths.

Source: CDC 1999

◀ Q U E S T I O N

5   ## A) 5,000 to 1

Believe it or not, some of the folks who remember World War I may still be around for World War III. Though they're still a relative rarity, about 60,000 Americans are now 100 years or older. That means there are more than 160 centenarians celebrating birthdays every day—enough to keep Willard Scott and his Smucker's jars on air for the *entire Today show!*
Source: U.S. Census Bureau 2004

◀ Q U E S T I O N

6   ## C) 4 to 1

So many women who have their implants taken out have them put back in right away that one has to wonder if there's some sort of thrill attached to the process. Maybe the second time around it's double-D pleasure.

Source: ASPRS 2004

◀ Q U E S T I O N

Losers—

7 The physical prowess of most men peaks in the late teens or early 20s. If you're a guy approaching 40, you're most likely to experience which of the following?

A) Hair Loss
B) Hearing Loss
C) Erectile Dysfunction

ANSWER ▶

The Sum of the Parts—

8 If you're an average, healthy American who dies in an accident, odds are you could help up to how many people by being an organ donor?

A) 25
B) 50
C) 110

ANSWER ▶

Going Down...or Up?

9 What are the odds that a plastic surgeon, on any given day, will perform breast augmentation surgery, compared to breast *reduction*?

A) 25 to 1
B) 12.5 to 1
C) 2.5 to 1

ANSWER ▶

7

A) Hair Loss

Yep! Fallout is probably your worst problem—at least for now—with 25 to 30% of men balding or seriously shedding by the time they're in their 20s. Despite what your mother said, hearing loss affects only about 14% of men in or near their 40s. And ED only about 5–10%—unless you're a heavy drinker or smoker, which could mean it's all downhill from here.

Source: CDC; NHS 2002

◀ Q U E S T I O N

8

B) 50

Since everything from hearts to corneas can now be successfully transplanted, a single donor could help as many as 50 other folks. An impressive 55% of the adult U.S. population list themselves as donors, with a few brave, living donors giving nonessential kidneys and bone marrow. *(These stats don't include self-donated, previously detached organs—John Bobbitt, we're looking at you.)*

Source: NWIHC; ABCNews.com 2003

◀ Q U E S T I O N

9

C) 2.5 to 1

Corporate downsizing may be all the rage, but the boob tube volume in the U.S. is twice as likely to go up (over 260,000 augmentations) than down (about 105,000 reductions). What's not entirely clear is whether most reductions are in response to excessive natural endowments, augmentations that have outlived their "usefulness," or simply the desire to see one's shoes.

Source: ASPRS 2004

◀ Q U E S T I O N

Earning Straight AAs—

10 What's the chance that a heavy drinker in college could be classified as an alcoholic?

A) 1 in 2
B) 1 in 5
C) 1 in 10

ANSWER ▶

I.C.U...uuewwww!

11 What's your chance of contracting an infection while a patient in a hospital?

That's a Sick Question!

A) 1 out of 100
B) 1 out of 20
C) 1 out of 10

ANSWER ▶

A Little Wrong in the Tooth—

12 For the over-65 crowd, having teeth has replaced having tobacco as something to chew on. What are the chances that anyone in this age bracket has full or partial dentures?

A) 80%
B) 60%
C) 40%

ANSWER ▶

41

10 **B) 1 in 5**

Joe and Jane College might need to take it down a keg or two. Of the heavy drinkers—men consuming 5 consecutive drinks, women 4—20% could be classified as alcoholics, compared to only 5% of the overall college student population. To make matters worse, only 6% of students with alcohol dependence reported that they'd sought treatment; presumably, the other 94% sought another round.

Source: Harvard School of Public Health 2002

◄ QUESTION

11 **C) 1 out of 10**

Cleanliness may be next to godliness, but it's apparently a very long way from the average ER. Nearly 10% of hospital patients will contract a disease or infection during their hospital stays, contributing to an estimated 20,000 or more deaths every year! The question is, if you get sick in a hospital, where do you go? *Only Mary Baker Eddy knows for sure...*

Source: CDC 2004

◄ QUESTION

12 **B) 60%**

For the more than 35 million senior citizens in the U.S., losing most, if not all, of your teeth is nothing to laugh at. In addition, poorly fitting dentures greatly exacerbate more serious problems, since not chewing properly is one of the leading causes of choking deaths. Makes you want to floss a little more fervently, doesn't it?

Source: NHANESIII

◄ QUESTION

Th-th-thanks, F-f-folks...

13 What are the odds that the children of a parent with a history of stuttering will also stutter?

A) 10%
B) 30%
C) 60%

ANSWER ▶

Fenders, Benders, or Dead-Enders?

14 A white man aged 85 or older is 5 times more likely than the national average to do which of the following?

A) Crash His Car
B) Leave His Wife
C) Kill Himself

ANSWER ▶

Face-Off—

15 There comes a time when makeup just isn't enough. Of the following minimally invasive procedures, which is a woman *least* likely to undergo?

A) Botox
B) Chemical Peel
C) Microdermabrasion

ANSWER ▶

13   C) 60%

S-s-stuttering isn't *caused* by parents—just inherited from them. It's a neuromuscular disorder, not an emotional one—though it can lead to negative self-image problems. Among the estimated 3 million Americans who struggle with the problem, parents pass on their stuttering to about 10% of their d-d-daughters and 20% of their s-s-sons. *(What kind of a j-j-jerk wr-r-rote this q-q-question, anyway?)*

Source: American Psychiatric Assoc.;DSM-IV-TR;NSF

◀ Q U E S T I O N

14   C) Kill Himself

For every 100,000 white men 85 and older, about 59 commit suicide each year, compared to an average of 10.6 per 100,000 in the rest of the population. The car crash rate is high too, but dashboard periscopes—and extra seat cushions—might prove helpful. Few, it seems, try to leave their wives. They just can't run that fast.

Source: NIMH 2001; DOT

◀ Q U E S T I O N

15   C) Microdermabrasion

Although all 3 are among the most popular non-surgical procedures undergone by women, about 700,000 are microderm*abraised*, compared to almost 890,000 who are chemically peeled, and over 2.6 million who take the needle…(of Botox). Hair removal and collagen injections round out the top 5 female facial fortifiers.

Source: ASPRS 2004

◀ Q U E S T I O N

Vhat's Zzzz Problem?

16 What are the chances that an average American suffers from a sleep disorder, including sleep deprivation or excessive daytime sleepiness?

A) 1 in 5
B) 2 in 5
C) 3 in 5

ANSWER ▶

The Battle of Bowel Run—

17 During the Civil War, what were the chances of Union soldiers contracting diarrhea or dysentery?

Hold Your Fire!

A) 1 out of 2
B) 3 out of 4
C) 9 out of 10

ANSWER ▶

Eye, Caramba!

18 What are the odds that a 50-year-old will develop presbyopia, a.k.a. trouble seeing things close up?

A) Over 35%
B) Over 75%
C) Over 95%

ANSWER ▶

16   **A) 1 in 5**

Between 50 and 70 million Americans are affected by sleep disorders, not counting those kept awake by others with a disorder. But not to worry. If you're having trouble sleeping, I could simply read this sentence to you over and over. I could simply read this sentence to you over and over. *I could simply read this sentence to you...*

Source: NIH 2004

◀ Q U E S T I O N

17   **C) 9 out of 10**

Atlanta wasn't the only thing that was burning. Only five out of every thousand Union soldiers managed to sidestep these gastric disorders. The Confederate army didn't fare any better, which begs the question: Who were those five guys?

Source: civilwarhome.com

◀ Q U E S T I O N

18   **C) Over 95%**

Bring out the bifocals and grab a cane. Almost everyone will have trouble seeing close up as they age. It's due to a hardening of the lens inside the eye, and it affects men and women equally. Most will compensate by increasing the length of their arms. If you think that's funny, you're under 40. Just wait.

Source: NIH 2004

◀ Q U E S T I O N

Weed Whackers—

19 What are the chances that an American supports the legalization of marijuana for medical purposes?

A) 2 in 5
B) 3 in 5
C) 4 in 5

ANSWER ▶

Game, Set, Patch—

20 Your nephew just got a high-powered BB gun from your crazy brother-in-law. What's the chance of little Tommy injuring his eyes or someone else's with his new toy?

A) 24%
B) 12%
C) 6%

ANSWER ▶

A Walk in the Dark—

21 A sleepwalking episode is most likely to last approximately how long?

A) 6 Seconds
B) 60 Seconds
C) 6 Minutes

ANSWER ▶

19 **C) 4 in 5**

"Now this prescription indicates that Dr. Bong is your regular physician?" Though only 34% of Americans believe that pot should be legalized entirely, 80% would have no problem with releasing it for medical use. And no, that doesn't include watching *General Hospital* or playing *Operation—The Wacky Doctor Game*.

Source: Time; CNN

◄ Q U E S T I O N

20 **B) 12%**

Those odds might seem to be in little Tommy's favor, but consider this: Of the more than 21,000 yearly injuries caused by BB guns and other nonpowder guns, almost 2,500 are to the eye. And of those, 40% cause blindness. Maybe all those risk-averse adults in the film, *A Christmas Story* were right— "You'll shoot your eye out, kid!"

Source: U.S. Eye Injury Registry 2004

◄ Q U E S T I O N

21 **C) 6 Minutes**

The average sleepwalker wanders woozily for about 6 minutes at a stretch, a time in which a very fit somnambulist could run at least a mile. However, if you bump into a "sleepwalker" whose flesh seems to be rotting off his body as he moans "Brains...brains," you might want to do a little running yourself.

Source: health.allrefer.com

◄ Q U E S T I O N

Nailed by a Tiny Prick—

22 Rusty nails, knives, and other implements which prick, scratch, or deeply puncture your body can lead to tetanus. In a typical year, if you live in the U.S., what is your chance of contracting this disease?

A) 1 in 68,000
B) 1 in 680,000
C) 1 in 6,800,000

ANSWER ▶

Urine...For a Good Night's Sleep—

23 Of the following, who is most likely to wet the bed?

Who Gives a Sheet?

A) A Child Aged 4
B) A Grandmother Aged 75
C) A Baby Chimpanzee

ANSWER ▶

Weight Class?

24 A man is likeliest to be overweight if he is in which of the following income levels?

A) $10–29,999
B) $30–49,999
C) $50,000+

ANSWER ▶

49

22   C) 1 in 6,800,000

Because the vast number of children and adults in the
U.S. are vaccinated against tetanus, we can all rest easier
on our bed of nails: only about 40 people a year contract
the dreaded disease. This contrasts appreciably with over
200,000 lockjaw victims worldwide who are asphyxiated,
convulse, and die.

Source: The World Health Report, WHO 2004; CDC 2004

◀ Q U E S T I O N

23   A) A Child Aged 4

If you're wondering who should get those rubber sheets this
Christmas, think little Timmy before Grandma Pearl. Studies
have shown that 85% of children may wet their beds before
age 5, while about 50% of the elderly have the same problem.
As for baby chimps, well, most of them don't sleep in
beds, Bonzo!

Source: Provident Medical Institute 2001; AAFP 1998

◀ Q U E S T I O N

24   C) $50,000+

The highest income group of American men are actually
more likely to be overweight than poor ones, while the opposite holds true for women, a trend that gives credence to
that whole Jack Sprat paradigm.

Source: National Center for Health Statistics 2004

◀ Q U E S T I O N

The Bourbon Dynasty—

25   A child of an alcoholic who is adopted away at birth is how much likelier than an average child to develop alcohol dependence?

A) Just as Likely
B) 3 to 4 Times as Likely
C) 12 to 15 Times as Likely

ANSWER ▶

At a Loss?

26   Most experts agree that America is in the midst of an obesity crisis. What are the chances of finding a diet book among the top 10 bestsellers?

A) Zero
B) 1 in 10
C) 2 in 10

ANSWER ▶

Out of Sight—

27   What are the chances that a blind person was born without sight?

A) 90%
B) 60%
C) 35%

ANSWER ▶

25   **B) 3 to 4 Times as Likely**

Adopted doesn't necessarily mean adapted. Even when removed from an alcoholic environment, the children of alcoholics still run a much greater risk of addiction problems than their less genetically predisposed peers. So, if it was love-at-first-sip, you might want to consider quitting before you become permanently attached.

Source: APA; DSM-IV-TR

◀ Q U E S T I O N

26   **C) 2 in 10**

Tens of millions of diet books have been sold in the U.S. in recent years. Today it's the *South Beach* franchise with two in the top ten, but over the years we've also fallen for low-carbs, no-carbs, Dr. Atkins, and The Zone. Still we're fat—and apparently getting fatter! Come on people, you've got to actually *read* these things *and deprive* yourselves...
Jane Fonda, where are you when we *need* you?
Source: U.S. Census Bureau 2004

◀ Q U E S T I O N

27   **C) 35%**

The blinding truth is that most unsighted people weren't always that way. Of the two-thirds born sighted, at least half lost their eyesight due to disease, and most of the others due to injury. *(The moral—eyesight is a gift, so don't take it for granted. You know, like you did with your sex life before you got married.)*

Source: Provident Medical Institute 2001; AAFP 1998

◀ Q U E S T I O N

Not to Be Rash...

28 Allergy sufferers are most likely to be allergic to which of the following fruits?

A) Bananas
B) Apples
C) Richard Simmons

ANSWER ▶

More-mones—

29 An average birth control pill in 1960 was likely to contain how much estrogen compared to a modern-day pill?

Ask Any 45-Year-Old!

A) Twice as Much
B) Five Times as Much
C) Twenty Times as Much

ANSWER ▶

Inferior Posterior—

30 What are your odds of getting hemorrhoids?

A) 1 to 1
B) 3 to 1
C) 10 to 1

ANSWER ▶

28   A) Bananas

Allergy suffers may experience cross reactivity, which makes them allergic to certain fruits. Of these, bananas are among the most common. An allergic reaction to Richard Simmons, on the other hand, is characterized by the inability to sweat to the oldies, a sudden lowering of volume, and in severe cases, the temptation to shut off the television altogether.

Source: American Academy of Allergy, Asthma and Immunology 2002

◄ Q U E S T I O N

29   B) Five Times as Much

Talk about a blast from the past! With 500% of today's estrogen dosage, the original birth control pills were crude but effective. Unfortunately, they were also effective at putting women at risk for blood clots, heart attacks, and strokes.

Source: Brown Univ., Health Ed.

◄ Q U E S T I O N

30   A) 1 to 1

You might as well begin your preparation for this affliction now. Though surveys vary, the Mayo Clinic gives even odds of contracting hemorrhoids over the course of a lifetime. Hemorrhoids may be the reason Hemingway wrote standing up—and in very short sentences. *(That somewhat meaningless, alliterative, literary connection aside, does anyone know why hemorrhoids aren't called asteroids?)*

Source: Mayo Clinic; Hemorrhoid.net

◄ Q U E S T I O N

Not Having a Ball!

31 Hey, guys! If you discover a lump where your balls should be—and it turns out to be cancer—you're most likely to have which of the following procedures?

A) Radiation Treatment
B) One Gonad Removed
C) Two Gonads Removed

ANSWER ▶

Doc-in-the-Box?

32 According to a new study, patients are more likely to be comfortable being treated by which?

Say, "Ahhh!"

A) A New Doctor, in Person
B) Regular Doctor, via Robot
C) A Witch Doctor

ANSWER ▶

Fourth of July Blast—

33 The chance is 1 in 4 that a fireworks-related accident will cause serious injury to which of the following?

A) Eyes
B) Hands
C) Toilet Bowls

ANSWER ▶

31 B) One Gonad Removed

You'll be relieved to know that in most cases only one has to go. And, the cure rate for testicular cancer, when treated early, is about 95%. So remember, while you're down there, take time out to check for lumps. The prospect of having your nuts cut off isn't a good one, but dying to keep them is even worse. Do it right, and you might be touring France like Lance Armstrong.

Source: NCI; SEER 2004; TCRC 2004

◀ QUESTION

32 B) Their Regular Doctor, via Robot

After being treated by video-robot doctors, known as "telerounds," 57% of patients decided they'd feel more comfortable with a robo-doc than a new, in-the-flesh physician. No word on whether the robots take a *Hippomatic* oath.

Source: MSNBC.com

◀ QUESTION

33 B) Hands

These mini-explosives cause about 6,900 accidents a year—sending 1,800 people to emergency clinics with burns, fractures, and contusions on their hands. Another 1,400 have eye injuries—some of them blinding. The other 3,700 injuries are to legs, trunks, arms, and shoulders. *(As for problems in the toilet, those of you responsible know who you are!)*

Source: CPSC 2003

◀ QUESTION

3

Love
&
Marriage

Is there someone for you out in cyberspace? When are you most likely to get engaged or married...and where will you go on your honeymoon? Are you more or less likely to marry someone you've lived with? What are the odds of a marriage lasting five years or fifty...or ending in divorce?

What are the chances you'll remarry or end up widowed?

From dating to divorcing and trying again, you'll find it all in Love & Marriage.

Kin Do—

1 If you live in the U.S. and want to marry your first cousin, what are the chances it would be legal?

A) 3 in 50
B) 11 in 50
C) 19 in 50

ANSWER ▶

Call Girls—

2 What are the chances that an American woman has asked a man out on a date?

Operators Standing By!

A) 4 in 10
B) 6 in 10
C) 8 in 10

ANSWER ▶

Out of Cyberia?

3 What's the likelihood that single adults (18+) with Internet access have visited an online dating site at least once?

A) 1 in 10
B) 3 in 10
C) 5 in 10

ANSWER ▶

1 **C) 19 in 50**

You can add family unions to reunions in 19 states and the District of Columbia. In fact, you can bump the number up to 27 if you don't mind a few restrictions (no children; genetic counseling, etc.) Or, if you're a man you could say screw all that and move to Saudi Arabia. There, 30 to 80% of marriages are between first cousins—so you could bring a lot more of the family into your tent with your 2nd, 3rd, and 4th wives.

Source: cousintocousin.com 2003

◀ QUESTION

2 **A) 4 in 10**

Despite some radical changes in gender relations, less than half of U.S. women have ever asked a man out on a date. But come on, girls—given the 93% (!) acceptance rate, it's certainly worth a try.

Source: Investor's Business Daily, Christian Science Monitor

◀ QUESTION

3 **B) 3 in 10**

It's the biggest revolution since The Dating Game! About 28% have reported visiting a dating site, and 16% report knowing someone whose Internet dating connection led to marriage. But most people (about 40%) think meeting through the Internet is even less safe than meeting in a bar. We're not sure, but it seems safer to get drunk and wake up the next morning with nothing but your keyboard beside you.

SOURCE: CBS News Poll 2003

◀ QUESTION

The Anti-Dutch Lobby—

4 What are the chances that women *and* men in the U.S. think a man should pay for a date?

A) 35 in 100
B) 55 in 100
C) 75 in 100

ANSWER ▶

Evasive Inaction—

5 Men are known for being a little slower to make marital commitments than women. What's the chance that a man will be married by the time he's 27?

A) 1 in 3
B) 1 in 5
C) 1 in 7

ANSWER ▶

Trial Runs—

6 What are the chances that an unmarried couple in the U.S. tries living together before tying the knot?

A) 35 in 100
B) 55 in 100
C) 75 in 100

ANSWER ▶

4   **A) 35 in 100**

Gentlemen, start your wallets! About 35% of Americans still
think it's the man's job to flash the cash on a date—whatever
the circumstances. And for first dates, "guys pay" rises to 43%.

Source: Investor's Business Daily

◀ Q U E S T I O N

5   **A) 1 in 3**

With most women good-to-go at 25, there seems to be
some foot-dragging going on here, guys. Of course, between
carousing and career, it's tough to fit in commitment—
especially when it involves the "f" word...*Forever* !

SOURCE: U.S. Census 1999

◀ Q U E S T I O N

6   **B) 55 in 100**

Almost 60% do, before they say "I do." Of those, about 40%
are married in two years, and 60% eventually get married.
But the divorce rate (already close to a flip-of-the-coin 50%)
is about 50% higher than the norm for couples who've co-
habited. Maybe it's just too much of a good thing.

Source: Center for Marital & Family Studies/U. Denver

◀ Q U E S T I O N

Free to Be?

7 Most Americans date and have the freedom to choose the person they wish to marry. But worldwide, what are the chances that a marriage is arranged?

A) 20%
B) 40%
C) 60%

ANSWER ▶

Rules of Engagement—

8 It's most likely that a couple in the U.S. will be engaged to be married for about how long?

Time to Find Your Altar Ego!

A) 6 Months
B) 11 Months
C) 16 Months

ANSWER ▶

Rating the Rock—

9 Your odds for a top-dollar valuation on a diamond are best if it has which of the following clarity grades?

A) FL
B) VS1
C) I-3

ANSWER ▶

7 **C) 60%**

Marriages in most of the world are still governed by custom and economics, and the choice of one's life partner is made by the parents, or the families, not by the couple. But then, what could be more exciting than sleeping with a stranger?

Source: Penguin Atlas of Human Sexual Behavior *2004*

◀ Q U E S T I O N

8 **C) 16 Months**

This is longer than a lot of marriages! The average engagement has gone from 11 months in 1990 to 16 months in 2002. Delay factors for today's elaborate weddings include up to a year's advance bookings for clergymen, place, band, photographer, etc. Then, too—with over 40% of you already living together—there isn't quite the same sense of urgency as in your parents' day.

Source: Condé Nast Bridal Infobank 2003; USA Today 2003

◀ Q U E S T I O N

9 **A) FL**

The "FL" is "Flawless." So, girls, if you get one of these gems—in addition to your smart, thoughtful fiancé—you've got a really fine "best friend!" The VS1 is pretty good, but like a lot of us, its small inclusions are visible under 10 times magnification. A I-3 is the lowest clarity rating. If you're the recipient of one of these, you might want to reconsider the whole thing.

Source: NY Diamond Exchange 2005; Diamond.com

◀ Q U E S T I O N

A Matter of Months—

10 Of the 2.4 million weddings annually in the U.S., June still tops the other months for the most weddings. Which of the following is the most likely runner-up?

A) October
B) August
C) September

ANSWER ▶

States of Matrimony—

11 Odds are that a wedding is most likely to take place In which of the following places?

Looking for Love!

A) Las Vegas, Nevada
B) Istanbul, Turkey
C) Gatlinburg, Tennessee

ANSWER ▶

It Costs <u>How Much</u>?

12 In the "gilding the lily" category, brides are spending more and more on wedding dresses. Odds are that an "average" wedding gown today will cost how much?

A) $400
B) $600
C) $800

ANSWER ▶

10 · B) August

August follows June's 11% with a little over 10% of all weddings. September (9.6%) and October (9.4%) are close runners-up. But come on, people, are you lemmings? To avoid the booking problems and higher prices, may we humbly suggest January? With less than 5% of U.S. weddings, it's been woefully neglected—and in most places it's got great weather for *indoor* activities!

Source: Modern Bride *2004*

◀ Q U E S T I O N

11 · B) Istanbul, Turkey

Congratulate those Turks for hosting 166,000 weddings in a year! Vegas hosted 114,000 in between turns at the slots. Gatlinburg, with 42,000, rated third. Guess you really can't keep 'em down on the farm, after they've seen...*Istanbul?*

Source: Modern Bride *2004*

◀ Q U E S T I O N

12 · C) $800

And that's just for the dress! With a 50% cost increase in weddings over the past ten years to an average of $20,000+, that walk down the aisle might also be into bankruptcy for whoever's picking up the tab. Cynics think the situation is out of control—but admirers have been heard to say *"Forget the cake, let's eat the bride!"*

Source: Modern Bride *2004*

◀ Q U E S T I O N

We're Outta Here—

13 Niagara Falls and the Poconos have long since been surpassed as hot spots for American honeymooners. Where in the world are today's newlyweds *most likely* to end up?

A) On a Cruise
B) A Domestic Location
C) A Foreign Location

ANSWER ▶

How Many Times?

14 For some, the honeymoon never ends. What are the odds that a married couple is sexually "engaged" four or more times a week?

A) 3%
B) 7%
C) 11%

ANSWER ▶

Shooting Blanks?

15 If you're a guy wanting to have kids, enthusiasm and all the right operating equipment might not be enough. What are the chances that a male will be the infertile member of the couple?

A) 10%
B) 20%
C) 40%

ANSWER ▶

13   **C) A Foreign Location**

Sixty-three percent of American newlyweds leave the
mainland for a "foreign" experience; 10% go cruising, leaving
37% of you "at home" in today's top domestic honeymoon
hot spots: Las Vegas, Hawaii, and (no jokes, please) the
Virgin Islands.

Source: Condé Nast Bridal Infobank 2004

◀ QUESTION

14   **B) 7%**

Guess we can call these seven-percenters "lucky in love"!
But 43% of men and 47% of women say they're in action only
a "few times" a month; and 3% of women and 1% of men
say they do without *entirely*. Which goes to prove you can't
please all of the people all of the time...*and some people
don't even bother.*

Source: Kinsey Institute 2002

◀ QUESTION

15   **C) 40%**

Guys can hump themselves silly, but male infertility is
responsible for 40% or more of couples' infertility. The
variety of causes include low, or no, sperm count, an
obstruction, or something called "retrograde ejaculation"—
that's when those little guys swim in the wrong direction,
ending up in the bladder, where, if they are not immediately
recovered, they get *really pissed*.

Source: National Center for Health Statistics 2001

◀ QUESTION

Leave, If You Get Pregnant—

16

Odds are that you'll receive at least some paid maternity leave if you become pregnant while employed in which country?

A) Russia
B) Saudi Arabia
C) United States

ANSWER ▶

Hail Caesar!

17

What's the chance that a baby will be delivered through a Cesarean section?

That Little Cut-up!

A) 1 in 4
B) 1 in 6
C) 1 in 10

ANSWER ▶

Kid Pro Quo—

18

There's good evidence that breast-fed babies are generally healthier, with greater immunity to childhood diseases. In which of the following states would a baby be most likely to be breast-fed?

A) Arkansas
B) Texas
C) Vermont

ANSWER ▶

16   A) Russia

It may be cold, but when it comes to mamushka, the Russians are warm at heart. Even today, Russian women get 28 weeks paid maternity leave by law, compared to 12 weeks unpaid in the U.S. (if you meet certain conditions), and nothing at all in Saudi Arabia. Of course, most Saudi women probably aren't allowed jobs to leave in the first place.

Source: Child Policy International 2001; U.S. PDA

◀ Q U E S T I O N

17   A) 1 in 4

The trend has been growing over the years and now a full 25% of all babies are delivered through Cesarean section. What would Caesar think if he knew that his name was synonymous with a large salad and a surgical procedure, albeit misspelled?

Source: www.childbirth.org/section/CSFAQ.html

◀ Q U E S T I O N

18   C) Vermont

Only about 55% of kids in Arkansas are part of this feeding program. (Not sure if that included "Bubba," but we suspect probably not.) Texas is in at the higher end with 66–75% breast-fed. (Not sure about "W" either, but again, probably not.) With over 75% participation, Vermont is in the top tier of breast-feeding states—a good chance for Ben & Jerry to add a new flavor to their lineup.

Source: Nat'l Immunization Survey/CDC 2003

◀ Q U E S T I O N

Matching Pairs?

19   If a woman has already had one set of fraternal twins without artificial help, what are her chances of having another set, compared to the average woman?

A) 2 Times as Likely
B) 4 Times as Likely
C) 6 Times as Likely

ANSWER ▶

Tell-a-Tubby—

20   Who's least likely to recognize that a child is obese?

A Fat Chance!

A) Dad
B) Mom
C) Pediatrician

ANSWER ▶

Can I Scratch That for You?

21   Of first-time married couples headed for divorce, the final breakup is most likely to come in which of the following years?

A) 3 Years
B) 7 Years
C) 11 Years

ANSWER ▶

19   B) 4 Times as Likely

Women who bear fraternal twins often have a pattern of releasing more than one egg per cycle and, therefore, a better chance of having another set—a great shortcut to your own in-house soccer team, although a bit overwhelming when contemplating college tuition.

Source: About.com; nomotci.org 2003

◀ Q U E S T I O N

20   A) Dad

According to a British study, a third of moms and 57% of dads failed to recognize that their little ones were anything but perfect. *Kind of the same way they view themselves.*

Source: MSNBC.com

◀ Q U E S T I O N

21   B) 7 Years

Apparently, it's still the *Seven-Year Itch*—as in the film, not the band—that does in the most marriages. The average length of marriages ending in divorce in the U.S. is almost 7.8 years for men and 7.9 years for women. *There must be a lot of you folks out there not scratching in the right place!*

Source: Divorce Magazine *statistics 2002*

◀ Q U E S T I O N

Cheat Sheets?

22   In any given year, what is the chance that
someone who's married will begin an extra-
marital affair?

A) 1 in 10
B) 1 in 20
C) 1 in 40

A N S W E R ▶

Pray Together...Stay Together?

23   "Holy matrimony" sounds good at the
ceremony, but who's listening? The chance
of divorce is lowest among couples who
classify their religious beliefs as which
of the following?

A) Christian
B) Jewish
C) Atheist

A N S W E R ▶

No Such Thing as No-Fault—

24   When a marriage breaks up, what is
the chance that the husband initiated
the divorce?

A) 1 Out of 2
B) 1 Out of 3
C) 2 Out of 3

A N S W E R ▶

22 **B) 1 in 20**

Less than 5% of Americans say they've cheated on their spouses in the last 12 months. But over a lifetime, the adultery rate jumps to almost 20%. So, make sure your mate is too enamored—*or intimidated*—to even consider such a romp, or keep that divorce lawyer on speed-dial.

Source: University of Chicago 2001

◀ Q U E S T I O N

23 **C) Atheist**

Whereas 1 in 3 Jewish and Christian couples break their vows by divorcing, the numbers seem to indicate that atheists—at 1 in 5— have a greater belief in maintaining their marriages than avowed religious folks. Either that, or atheists simply don't believe in going through the hell of getting divorced.

Source: Barna Research Group 1999

◀ Q U E S T I O N

24 **B) 1 Out of 3**

Women initiate two-thirds of all divorces. Which means the guys are perfectly fine with the way things are—or maybe not. *(See how you can manipulate statistics!)*

Source: http://marriage.rutgers.edu/Publications/pubtoptenmyths.htm

◀ Q U E S T I O N

That Trophy Time of <u>Wife</u>?

25   Some think of it as "trading up" and for others it's the only way to get it up. What's the chance that a man over 45 will divorce his wife to marry a much younger woman?

A) 1 in 5
B) 1 in 10
C) 1 in 45

ANSWER ▶

Separation in State—

26   After all is said and done, in which state are you most likely to get divorced?

Idaho, but Alaska!

A) New York
B) California
C) Nevada

ANSWER ▶

Second Chances?

27   First-time marrieds currently have about a 50-50 shot of making the marriage work. What are the chances that a second marriage will end in divorce?

A) 40%
B) 60%
C) 80%

ANSWER ▶

25 **B) 1 in 10**

Those new models in the showroom can sure turn a guy's head—especially if the old model hasn't been giving good service. Of course, the cost of one of those zippy new things can be prohibitively expensive by the time you pay to get rid of the old one and do what you'll have to do to keep the new one running smoothly.

Source: American Sexual Behavior, National Opinion Research Center 1998

◄ Q U E S T I O N

26 **C) Nevada**

What goes there doesn't always stay there—especially where marriage is concerned. New York's divorce rate is about one-fourth of Nevada's; and California's rate is less than one-third. Of course, Nevada does allow "quickie" divorces, so some of their excess is from out-of-staters. Still, one has to wonder after those touching, Vegas wedding chapel vows, *how did it all go wrong?*

Source: U.S. Census Bureau 2000

◄ Q U E S T I O N

27 **B) 60%**

Experience can be a great teacher if you actually learn from your mistakes. If you're in that 40% minority who makes it work, go straight to the head of the wedded class. For the rest of you, it's back to the lawyers.

Source: CDC; U.S. Census 2002

◄ Q U E S T I O N

If the Pants Fit—

28 Among U.S. married couples, what are the chances that a wife earns over $5,000 a year more than her husband?

A) 5 in 100
B) 15 in 100
C) 35 in 100

ANSWER ▶

Golden Oldies?

29 What is the chance of a married couple reaching their golden wedding anniversary?

And Who Remembers?

A) 1 in 40
B) 1 in 20
C) 1 in 10

ANSWER ▶

Till Death Do They Part—

30 It's no secret that women generally outlive men, although the gap is narrowing. What are the odds a woman will be widowed compared to those of a man becoming a widower?

A) 4 to 1
B) 6 to 1
C) 8 to 1

ANSWER ▶

28　**B) 15 in 100**

Fifteen percent of wives are now the primary wage earners
in the family. And in unmarried-partner households the
proportion of female breadwinners is even higher—22%.
But overall, women's income as a proportion of men's has
risen only 10%…in the last 50 years! *(Did someone say, "glass
ceiling," again?)*

Source: Factmonster.com

◀ Q U E S T I O N

29　**B) 1 in 20**

Whether they're still madly in love or just gluttons for
punishment—5 out of every 100 married couples are
surviving the marriage minefield—and old age—to celebrate
their 50th wedding anniversaries. And they're celebrating in
style, creating a mini-growth market for event venues and all
things "50th!" from cards to cakes to gold Depends. *Here's
looking at you, kids!*

Source: Divorce Magazine *statistics 2002; CDC 2001; Cowles Bus. Media*

◀ Q U E S T I O N

30　**A) 4 to 1**

Whether they're loving them to death or working them into
an early grave, widows (women) still outnumber widowers
(men) 11 million to 2.6 million. Women living longer doesn't
quite account for the huge differential, though the stats on
the number of older guys with younger wives surely would.

Source: CDC; U.S. Census 2002

◀ Q U E S T I O N

We Didn't Miss the Bliss... Did We?

4

Sex & Sinners

"Women need a reason to have sex. Men need a place."
— NORA EPHRON —

We've got the odds on who's making it or faking it. Who's coming too soon...or not at all.

What are those teens really up to? And is granny really getting it on?

From sexual preferences to perversions—it's all in the numbers. Take a look and test yourself.

Odds are you'll be amazed.

Solo Flights—

1   Masturbation has been around since the beginning of recorded time. After all, the essentials are always "at hand." What are the chances that a guy has regularly availed himself of this pleasure principle compared to those of a girl?

A) 6 to 1
B) 3 to 1
C) 2 to 1

ANSWER ▶

Eager Beavers?

2   If the "sweet sixteen" of today is the "twenty-something" of the last generation, what are the chances that today's teenage girl has had sex (yes, intercourse) *before* her 15th birthday?

A) 13 in 100
B) 21 in 100
C) 33 in 100

ANSWER ▶

Priss-Teens?

3   With the bare teen midriffs, pierced navels, and model makeup everywhere in evidence, it's tempting to think teenage girls are in full sexual swing. What's the likelihood that girls 15–17 *have not* had sexual intercourse?

A) 10%
B) 30%
C) 70%

ANSWER ▶

1   **C) 2 to 1**

With 60% of guys and 30% of girls going it alone, it's a wonder population growth hasn't stopped altogether—a likely reason for masturbation's prohibition in many societies. But so far, we've found no evidence of hairy palms, blindness, or insanity attributable to it—even if practiced on a regular basis. Just remember when you lock that door, you're not fooling anybody.

Source: Kinsey Institute 2002

◀ Q U E S T I O N

2   **A) 13 in 100**

Surprise! This 13% actually represents almost a *50% decline* from the 1995 level of 19%. (Sorry, guys.) But moms and dads can take heart—whether it's fear or principle, something's working. Maybe you won't have to keep them locked up until they're 21.

Source: "Teenagers in the U.S. Sexual Activity, Contraceptive Use, and Childbearing" 2002

◀ Q U E S T I O N

3   **C) 70%**

They may be into other means of sexual gratification, but an amazing 70% of 15- to17-year-olds say they haven't done "it"—yet.

Source: People magazine and the Today show 2005

◀ Q U E S T I O N

Lip Service?

4   What are the odds that teen girls don't consider oral sex as "having sex" at all?

A) 38%
B) 58%
C) 78%

ANSWER ▶

Beginner's Luck!

5   For most teens, parenting is not the planned outcome of their sexual experimentation. But it happens. What are the chances that a teen pregnancy was planned?

A) 3%
B) 12%
C) 18%

ANSWER ▶

Retro-Sexual—

6   In 1988, 61% of girls 15 to 19 reported having had two or more sexual partners. What were the chances that their 1910 counterparts had been "intimate" with more than one heterosexual partner before marriage?

A) 1.5%
B) 3.3%
C) 12.5%

ANSWER ▶

4　**A) 38%**

Are these girls just paying "lip service" to the idea of virginity? Maybe. But at least 47% of teen boys agree. Of course, 80% of the oral sex was gal-on-guy, so the guys certainly have a vested interest in keeping the illusion alive.

Source: People *magazine and the* Today *show 2005*

◀ Q U E S T I O N

5　**B) 12%**

Of the 425,493 teen pregnancies in 2002, only about 1 in 8 was "planned"—by at least one of the participants. For the other 88% the pregnancy was an "unintended surprise." Now that's not something to call your kid, but it sure beats "Get over here, you little bastard!" *(And FYI, boys and girls, you can get pregnant "the first time.")*

Source: "Teenagers in the U.S. Sexual Activity, Contraceptive Use, and Childbearing" 2002

◀ Q U E S T I O N

6　**B) 3.3%**

"He won't buy the cow if he's getting the milk for free." With that oft-repeated admonition ringing in her ears, along with the fear of pregnancy and a ruined reputation, most girls in 1910 went into marriage—for better or worse—with no sexual experience.

Source: American Sexual Behavior, National Opinion Research Center 1998

◀ Q U E S T I O N

Come Prepared—

7   Okay, scouts! If you're a teenage boy making your first foray into the "sexual unknown," what are the chances you'll be using a condom?

A) 28%
B) 65%
C) 82%

A N S W E R ▶

Calendar That!

8   If you're in your 40s, you're most likely to have sex how many times during the year?

Leap Years Included!

A) 34 Times
B) 64 Times
C) 84 Times

A N S W E R ▶

Magic Moment—

9   Odds are that most Americans will have sex at what time tonight?

A) 9:34 p.m.
B) 10:34 p.m.
C) 11:34 p.m.

A N S W E R ▶

7   C) 82%

Merit badges all around! The rubbers roll out for about four-fifths of guys on their virgin voyage. An impressive example of premeditation, or simple preparedness. Either way a good showing. (Of course, that still leaves almost 20% of you exposed…to AIDS and a long list of STDs, not to mention fatherhood.)

Source: "Teenagers in the U.S. Sexual Activity, Contraceptive Use, and Childbearing" 2002

◀ Q U E S T I O N

8   B) 64 Times

Not very encouraging if you're a 40-something. But you're only 20 under the 18 to 29 crowd at 84 times, and you're *way ahead* of your elders, so enjoy it while you can. After 70, you'll likely be down to about ten times a year—no doubt skipping a couple of months to recuperate.

Source: Kinsey Institute 2002

◀ Q U E S T I O N

9   B) 10:34 p.m.

Maybe prime time TV just isn't holding viewers' attention—or maybe the commercial breaks are now long enough to get it on *and over with* before the televised action starts again—but 10:34 p.m. is the number one nookie nexus among the largest number of amorous Americans.

Source: The Andrology Institute

◀ Q U E S T I O N

Petrified!

10
It's the feeling a guy gets when his "woody" goes from wonderful to rock solid for four or more hours—and *won't let up!* It's called priapism, and males are most likely to have it if they have which of the following?

A) A Few Joints
B) Sickle-Cell Anemia
C) Too Much Viagra

ANSWER ▶

Time Zone—

11
Hey, guys. If you live to love, your best odds for "going a full half hour" are with someone from which country?

Crossing the International Dateline!

A) Brazil
B) Thailand
C) United States

ANSWER ▶

Measuring Up—

12
If there's anything that really worries guys—other than impotence and pregnancy—it's the size of their penis. The most likely size for an adult man— *at attention*— is which of the following?

A) 3–4″
B) 5–7″
C) 8–11″

ANSWER ▶

10   B) Sickle-Cell Anemia

A guy's dream of being "a man of steel" is a nightmare when the side effect is an erection that just won't quit—even after sex or a helping hand. It's particularly serious for black males with sickle-cell anemia—where 42% of the men and 64% of the young boys will have the problem. And it's no joke for those aroused by weed or an overreaction to those little blue pills—since episodes *can shrink and destroy your penis!*

Source: The Impotence Sourcebook. Dr. Christopher Steidle

◀ Q U E S T I O N

11   A) Brazil

Another reason to visit Rio! Those torrid Brazilians average 30 minutes per romantic interlude—the longest in the world. Americans come close, at 28 minutes, while Thais are the world's most efficient lovers, at an average of just 10 minutes per sexual encounter.

Source: Penguin Atlas of Human Sexual Behavior

◀ Q U E S T I O N

12   B) 5–7″

Relax, guys. Most of us aren't endowed with the "Long Dong Silver" of Clarence Thomas/Anita Hill fame, but we've got sufficient stature to make a good impression. And walking around with several extra inches dangling between your legs would seem to have its own set of problems. For those of you on the short end of the stick, well…enthusiasm and technique count for a lot…*really.*

Source: Kinsey Institute 2002; Human Sexual Behavior, J. Mackay

◀ Q U E S T I O N

Bent Out of Shape—

13 When a guy's "Mr. Happy" looks more like something the plumber would call a "bad connection," it's usually Peyronie's Disease. What's the chance this condition will mangle the member of someone you know?

A) 1 in 100
B) 1 in 1,000
C) 1 in 1,000,000

A N S W E R ▶

Whore-ific Experiences—

14 What are the chances that a juvenile arrested in the U.S. for prostitution or engaging in "commercialized vice" is male?

Can You Say Pedophile?!?

A) 25%
B) 35%
C) 45%

A N S W E R ▶

Faster Than a...

15 First-time sex gets lots of guys so excited that they lose control and ejaculate prematurely. What is the chance that a guy's virgin flight will end with a climax *at the beginning*?

A) 1 in 2
B) 1 in 4
C) 1 in 6

A N S W E R ▶

13   ## C) 1 in 1,000,000

Sounds rare, but there's a small army of 40- to 60-year-old guys out there in loose-fitting boxers hoping to go *undetected* when they get an erection. The deformity was discovered by French surgeon François de la Peyronie in 1743. There are surgical and nonsurgical treatments—but with something like this, you certainly don't want to take any shortcuts.

Source: urologychannel.com

◄ Q U E S T I O N

14   ## C) 45%

Boys comprise nearly half the nationwide prostitution arrests among juveniles, and most of their clients are *not* lonely married women—but *their husbands.*

Source: World-War-2.info

◄ Q U E S T I O N

15   ## B) 1 in 4

About 25% of males botch this the first time (and frequently thereafter) with a momentary experience that isn't shared by their sexual partners. Scientifically, it's hard to define what exactly constitutes "premature" since some men (and women) are happy with two, five, or ten minutes, while others are into record-setting performances. As long as you *both* finish—who's counting?

Source: Office of Juvenile Justice and Delinquency Prevention 2002

◄ Q U E S T I O N

A Roll in the Hay—

16 According to Dr. Alfred Kinsey's 1950s research, what percentage of farm boys reported having had "significant" sexual contact with an animal?

A) 1 Out of 100
B) 9 Out of 100
C) 17 Out of 100

ANSWER ▶

Pulsating Possibilities—

17 Not everything is natural, or real, even when it comes to sexual encounters. (Remember *M. Butterfly?*) Of the following choices, which has a 2 in 5 chance of occurring?

A) Woman's Faked Orgasm
B) Man's Faked Orgasm
C) Woman's Vibrator Use

ANSWER ▶

Gender Benders—

18 Life's a drag for a substantial population of people who, unlike gays, want to *be* the opposite sex. What's the chance that a male is transsexual?

A) 1 in 1,200
B) 1 in 12,000
C) 1 in 120,000

ANSWER ▶

16   **C) 17 out of 100**

That's right: 17% of '50s farm boys reported having *sexual* contact with the livestock—and it wasn't just "heavy petting"! More recent studies have shown a marked decrease in this form of "animal husbandry." In part, we guess, because the media reinforces unrealistic images of animals that are slim and pretty. *Or maybe with the decline of small farms, there just isn't enough privacy in the barn anymore.*

Source: Kinsey Institute 1953

◀ Q U E S T I O N

17   **A) Woman's Faked Orgasm**

About 40% of women are into this act. And almost 30% (age 25–34) own vibrators. Although there were no reports of gals faking it with their vibrators, neither of these findings reflect well on their partners' performances. (There were no reports of men faking orgasm.) The study was conducted by a condom maker and didn't consider lesbian liaisons. But it's worthy research if you want to volunteer!

Source: Durex Annual Sex Survey 2004

◀ Q U E S T I O N

18   **B) 1 in 12,000**

Could *this* be Victoria's Secret? Judging by the numbers, it's a pretty big party of gender dysphoric folks—though less than 30% of "cross-sex" males go through the arduous and expensive operations and hormone therapy that turns "Mikes" into "Micheles." Of the estimated 7,000–12,000 sex-change operations which have been performed in the U.S., they're about evenly split, M-T-F and F-T-M.

Source: Dr. M. Brown; Journal of Clinical Endocrinology & Metabolism 2003

◀ Q U E S T I O N

Granny Gets It On—

19

What is the chance that an American woman over the age of 75 has a sexual partner?

A) 1 in 2
B) 1 in 4
C) 1 in 10

ANSWER ▶

"Abstinent" About Sex?

20

The odds are that only 6% of which of these age groups reported having *no sexual intercourse* over the past year?

A) 18- to 29-year-olds
B) 30- to 39-year-olds
C) Over 70

ANSWER ▶

Smitten or Bitten?

21

Forget the whips and switches. What was the chance that males and females in the 1950s responded erotically to being bitten?

A) 1 in 10
B) 1 in 4
C) 1 in 2

ANSWER ▶

19   **B) I in 4**

Go, Granny, go! According to the AARP, about 25% of women over 75 have regular sexual partners. The rest are sticking with *"Not tonight, dear, I've had a heart attack."*

Source: AARP; myhealthyhorizon.com 2003

◄ Q U E S T I O N

20   **B) 30- to 39-year-olds**

At about 13%, the 18- to 29-year-olds had more than *double* the 30-somethings' 6% level of abstinence—either voluntary or not so. The over-70 crowd has a wistful 61% level of abstinence. But here's where those "senior moments" really come in handy—*you don't miss what you can't remember.*

Source: Kinsey Institute 1998

◄ Q U E S T I O N

21   **C) I in 2**

Wow! Fifty percent of males and 55% of females were aroused *by molars*. But before you sink your teeth in like those freewheeling '50s hipsters, be sure you're with a like-minded partner—*or a good dentist.*

Source: Kinsey Institute 1953

◄ Q U E S T I O N

Bound for Glory—

22 It takes more to get some people going than others. What's the chance that a guy is into bondage?

A) 3 in 100
B) 7 in 100
C) 11 in 100

ANSWER ▶

Bi-Ways—

23 Sexually, this isn't a matter of "being on the other team," but one of taking pitches from *both* sides of the plate. If you're bisexual, you're likeliest to be which of the following?

A) A Man
B) A Woman
C) Conflicted

ANSWER ▶

Let Me Count the Ways—

24 According to a recent poll, if you're an average American, you're *least* likely to have been sexually involved with which of the following?

A) A Different Race
B) The Same Sex
C) A Threesome

ANSWER ▶

22   ## C) 11 in 100

If you're a guy with this kink in your kit, you won't have trouble finding a playmate—or *two*. With 17 in 100 women also into this form of arousal, the odds are in your favor. *Cuffs, please...*

Source: Kinsey Institute 2002

◀ QUESTION

23   ## B) A Woman

Bi, Bi, Miss American Pie. There are about 1.5 times as many women who say they're bisexual than there are men—which could help even out the male-female ratio in the U.S., and makes these gals a guy's idea of heaven for a threesome. *(And if you picked "C—Conflicted," give yourself half a point).*

Source: Statistical Abstract of the U.S. 2001

◀ QUESTION

24   ## B) The Same Sex

While 40% have been involved with someone of a different race, and 18% *claim* to have been part of a threesome, only 6% of respondents reported trying it with someone of the same sex. *Of course, to be in a threesome, wouldn't at least two of you have to be of the same...oh well, never mind.*

Source: E! Online 2002

◀ QUESTION

The Iceman Cometh—

25   Not yet available at your local ATMs, sperm banking requires a very cold climate. What are the chances your deposit will survive their cryogenic journey from freezer to egg warmer?

A) 5% to 10%
B) 20% to 40%
C) 50% to 80%

ANSWER ▶

Blatant or Latent?

26   What are the chances that a woman who contracts chlamydia, a sexually transmitted disease, will be totally symptom-free?

A) 1 in 4
B) 2 in 4
C) 3 in 4

ANSWER ▶

Self-Contained—

27   Greek mythology tells of Hermaphroditus, a young man whose body was fused with his female lover by the gods. What is the chance of someone being born a hermaphrodite— with *both* male and female sex organs?

A) 1 in 125,000
B) 1 in 250,000
C) 1 in 375,000

ANSWER ▶

25   **C) 50% to 80%**

That -196°C temp is almost certain to freeze the tail off all but the heartiest of deposits. And submissions must be "viable." That requires about six vials and a helping hand. Although you can do this from home, it's recommended that you set up an appointment when you're ready—probably 24/7 for most guys.

Source: Reproductive Technologies, Inc. 2005

◀ Q U E S T I O N

26   **C) 3 in 4**

What you don't know can hurt you. Seventy-five percent of female chlamydia sufferers and 50% of men with the disease have no discernible symptoms at all. And that's particularly scary because, untreated, chlamydia can cause irreversible infertility by scarring of the fallopian tubes—a condition affecting an estimated 100,000 women a year in the U.S.

Source: STDs: What You Don't Know Can Hurt You, D. Yancey; NIAID 2004

◀ Q U E S T I O N

27   **B) 1 in 250,000**

There are an estimated 1,100 intersexuals (hermaphrodites) in the U.S. For anyone into group sex, this may seem like a free pass, but it's not nearly as much fun—or funny—as it sounds. *Plus, you have to be really, really careful not to get pregnant when you masturbate!*

Source: nih.gov

◀ Q U E S T I O N

Hot Flashes and Cold Sweats—

28 Strictly from a guy's point of view, it's most likely that a woman going through menopause is going to need which of the following?

A) Lubrication
B) Fortification
C) A Good Night's Sleep

ANSWER ▶

Lost That Lovin' Feeling?

29 Impotence makes guys who can't get it up, down and disheartened. What's the chance a guy in the U.S. has this problem?

A) 5-9%
B) 10-15%
C) 16-20%

ANSWER ▶

What Are They Praying For?

30 Call it the "Passion of the Churchgoers." Of those who attend religious services, which of the following is most likely to have had sex recently?

A) Rare Visitors
B) Occasional Visitors
C) Frequent Visitors

ANSWER ▶

28   **A) Lubrication**

If you're looking for a good time, take her to Jiffy Lube. The sweats and flashes are brief and intermittent, but the sex can go on indefinitely if you have the stamina and she has the K-Y Jelly.

Source: *American Sexual Behavior, National Opinion Research Center 1998*

◀ QUESTION

29   **B) 10-15%**

Depression, diabetes and a variety of other causes are rendering 12 to 20 million men in the U.S. impotent. And that, of course, affects not only the impotent, but also their partners, pals, and playmates. Fortunately there's a host of solutions—from pumps to those little blue pills—working to improve prospects for everyone.

Source: *National Kidney and Urologic Diseases Information Clearinghouse 1995*

◀ QUESTION

30   **A) Rare Visitors**

"Time in church" or "Time in bed?" The rare visitors are in at 66 times a year. The regular attendees, on the other hand, are likely to have sex on the weekly side—doing it an average of 51 times a year. The occasional visitors are in at 63. Seems like fodder for a "Sex for Sinners?" Sunday sermon in the works.

Source: *American Sexual Behavior, National Opinion Research Center 1998*

◀ QUESTION

Satisfied with
Your Performance?

5

Risky Business

> **"** The most dangerous thing in the world
> is to try to leap a chasm in two jumps. **"**
> — WILLIAM LLOYD GEORGE —

There's risk in everything you do—or <u>fail</u> to do! But some things are a little riskier than others.

What are the odds of surviving a skydiving jump...or a commercial plane crash?

Could you make it to the top of Mt. Everest? Or deal with Wild Bill Hickok's "Dead Man's Hand"?

Find out how well you deal with life's gambles in Risky Business!

Auto Pilot?

1 Young children are easily lulled to sleep by the motion of a car. In any given year, what's the chance of a driver falling asleep at the wheel?

A) 1 in 75
B) 1 in 12
C) 1 in 4

ANSWER ▶

Plane Terrifying—

2 The thought of the plane you're in falling out of the sky, or otherwise crashing, wouldn't give anybody on board much reason to hope. What are the odds of surviving a commercial plane crash?

A) Zero
B) 3 to 1
C) 3 to 2

ANSWER ▶

"Billy Bob—We're Movin' Again!"

3 Seems tornadoes are predisposed to trailer trashing. What are the chances that the state with the most tornadoes is also a top market for mobile homes?

A) 100%
B) 50%
C) 30%

ANSWER ▶

1   **C) 1 in 4**

WAKE UP!!! It's estimated that over 24,000 deaths and almost 2.5 million disabling injuries a year are caused by drowsy drivers—*almost a third more than those caused by drunk drivers!* When your eyelids start drooping, pull over! You're about to become your own worst nightmare—and everybody else's.

Source: National Sleep Foundation; MADD 2002

◀ Q U E S T I O N

2   **C) 3 to 2**

At almost 33%, the survival rate is a lot better than you might have thought—and probably better odds of survival than most airlines have right now. Add to that the 1 in 11 million chance that you'd ever be in a plane crash to begin with...and it really is the safest way to travel...*Really!*

Source: National Transportation Safety Board 2004

◀ Q U E S T I O N

3   **A) 100%**

The Hoosier (as in, "*Who's your insurance agent?*") state goes to the head of the class! Whether by bizarre coincidence or brilliant marketing, Indiana (with 36% of all tornado deaths) is ranked first in "danger from tornadoes" and in sales of mobile homes. (*No, Dorothy lived in a farmhouse in Kansas...* which ranks *third* for tornadoes.)

Source: FEMA 2002; Census of Mfgs/Industries; National Climatic Data Center

◀ Q U E S T I O N

Empire Building?

4

There are lots of ways to go bust in the first year of business. Based on the percentage of bankruptcies—by industry—in New York State, which of the following is the riskiest?

A) Plumbing
B) Trucking
C) Food Service/Restaurants

ANSWER ▶

On the Edge—

5

Today millions of U.S. kids are skateboarding and trampolining. What's the likelihood that a kid will end up in the ER from an injury on a skateboard compared to a trampoline?

A) Half as Likely
B) The Same
C) Twice as Likely

ANSWER ▶

Heads Up, Gramps!

6

Keeping fit has its own potential pitfalls. If you're over 50, what are the odds you'll be killed riding a bike, compared to those of a kid under 15?

A) 1 to 2
B) 1 to 1
C) 2 to 1

ANSWER ▶

4   A) Plumbing

With an 83% failure rate, the industry prize for "going down the drain" in the first year goes to the plumbers! Truckers ran a close second at 81%. Also folding fast were restaurants (79%); in fact, because of the large number of restaurant startups, the actual number of restaurant failures is almost double that of the other two industries combined. So, if you chose "C—Food Service," give yourself half a point.

Source: Business Week; NY Labor Dept. 2004

◀ Q U E S T I O N

5   A) Half as Likely

While ollying into action on a skateboard like Tony Hawk can land you on the pavement, skateboarders have only half of the 100,000 annual ER visits of trampoliners, and about one-third the fatalities. Of course, you can keep the kids indoors—in front of the TV or computer—where the likeliest things they'll stumble on are fatty foods and Internet pedophiles.

Source: U.S. Product Safety Commission 2002

◀ Q U E S T I O N

6   C) 2 to 1

Older can mean dumber—as in not wearing a helmet! That's the single biggest reason more adults are killed riding their bikes than kids are. So take a lesson from your grandkids. Helmets might not have been hip in your day, but neither was Viagra!

Source: U.S. Product Safety Commission 2002

◀ Q U E S T I O N

Cop Stops—

7 Every state but New Hampshire has mandatory seat belt laws. What's the annual chance, anywhere in the U.S. that an on-duty police officer's death in a car crash is attributable to not buckling up?

A) 1 in 3
B) 1 in 5
C) 1 in 10

ANSWER ▶

Yo Ho Ho...

8 A ship carrying valuable cargo is most likely to be attacked by pirates in which of the following waters?

Planning a Cruise?

A) Caribbean Sea
B) Aegean Sea
C) Indian Ocean

ANSWER ▶

Dead Man's Hand—

9 Wild Bill Hickok was killed holding pairs of black aces and black eights—hence the moniker, "Dead Man's Hand." We assume your odds of being shot at the poker table are minimal. What's the chance of being dealt this hand?

A) 1 in 59
B) 1 in 5,900
C) 1 in 59,000

ANSWER ▶

7   **A) 1 in 3**

Amazingly, more cops die in car crashes than at the hands of criminals—a third of the time simply because they didn't buckle their seat belts. And most of these crashes—over 60%—weren't in life-or-death chases, but in normal traffic. So next time you jump into your patrol cars remember that good-ole-boy saying, "My mama didn't raise no fools..." *Or did she?*

Source: U.S. Product Safety Commission 2002

◄ Q U E S T I O N

8   **C) Indian Ocean**

You probably haven't seen a ship flying the "Jolly Roger" since the last rerun of *Treasure Island*, but modern-day pirates are out there—armed with guns, machetes, Uzis, and dynamite. From the Caribbean and Aegean to the *most dangerous* waters around Indonesia (where 30 crew members were killed in 2004 alone), over 300 incidents of piracy are reported each year.

Source: Amnesty International 2005; National Geographic 2002

◄ Q U E S T I O N

9   **C) 1 in 59,000**

Not a likely draw, unless you're spending a whole lot of time at the poker table. Of course, Wild Bill probably would have traded the hand for better odds on living. And those might have improved significantly if he'd just kept his back to the wall (as was his habit) and hadn't already killed his murderer's brother. Another misstep? His choice of towns— *Deadwood, SD.*

Source: Britannica Almanac; S. Verhoeven 2005

◄ Q U E S T I O N

Mounting Challenges—

10

If you were to pull on your woolies, grab a few bottles of oxygen, and call for a Sherpa, what's the chance that you'd make it to the top of Mt. Everest, the world's tallest mountain and the highest point on the earth?

A) 1 to 3
B) 1 to 13
C) 1 to 23

ANSWER ▶

Leap of Faith!

11

There are about 350,000 skydivers in the U.S.—an extreme sport that requires know-how, trust, and at least a bit of lunacy. What are the odds that a skydiver *will survive* a leap?

A) 6,700 to 1
B) 67,000 to 1
C) 670,000 to 1

ANSWER ▶

Blowin' Smoke?

12

In addition to the unhappy prospect of developing lung cancer—*which now kills more women than breast cancer*—the odds are 12 to 1 that a woman who smokes also will do which of the following?

A) Die Prematurely
B) Have a Low-Weight Baby
C) Develop Heart Disease

ANSWER ▶

10   **C) 1 to 23**

At almost 30,000 feet, with only one-third of the oxygen at sea level, and covered by 5–20 feet of snow year-round, Everest has daunted all but 205 of the over 4,000 adventurous souls who have tried to reach its peak. Of the 140 who have perished in their attempts, 120 remain frozen somewhere on the mountain. The first conquest of the summit was in 1953, the most recent was in 2005. *What's on your vacation agenda?*

Source: Everest News; National Geographic; *Britannica.com*

◀ Q U E S T I O N

11   **B) 67,000 to 1**

These folks have overcome their fear of flying, falling—*at about 120 mph*—and dying! But with over 2 million jumps a year, and an average of about 30 fatalities, there are fewer deaths from skydiving than from scuba diving (90) or bee stings (46). Injuries can be serious, but only about 1,200 were reported to the USPA in 2002. And, about 4% of jumpers are over 60! *Wonder if that counts as a stress test?*

Source: U.S. Parachute Association 2002; Skydiving *magazine*; CDC

◀ Q U E S T I O N

12   **A) Die Prematurely**

In the U.S. 178,000 women die each year from lung cancer— mostly from smoking. The habit also doubles a woman's risk of coronary heart disease and other diseases, and accounts for 20 to 30% of low-birth-weight babies. In the words of the old Virginia Slims slogan, *"You've come a long way, baby, to get where you've got to today."* If you want to keep what you've got, *give it up!*

Source: American Lung Association 2004

◀ Q U E S T I O N

Battle Worn—

13 Over 40 million Americans have served in the military—from the Civil War to the present war in Iraq. Of the 3,460 who have received the Congressional Medal of Honor, what is the chance it was awarded posthumously?

A) 1 in 3
B) 1 in 6
C) 1 in 12

ANSWER ▶

De-Constructed—

14 When you're putting up a building, which of the following workers is most likely to "go down" on the job with a fatal injury?

Die-Hard Employees!

A) A Carpenter
B) A Roofer
C) An Electrician

ANSWER ▶

Wired?

15 The flying Wallendas were renowned for their family high-wire act with a seven-person pyramid. When one man lost his footing 25 feet above the ground, causing them to fall, what were the chances that anyone survived?

A) 3 in 7
B) 5 in 7
C) 6 in 7

ANSWER ▶

13   **B) 1 in 6**

Fortunately, 5 out of 6 recipients survived to personally
receive this honor for unusual valor in armed combat. There
have been 19 double recipients. The first recipients were 6
Americans involved in "The Great Locomotive Chase" in
1862. The most recent medal was awarded posthumously
to the family of Sgt. 1st Class, Paul R. Smith on April 4, 2005.

Source: Congressional Medal of Honor Society 2005

◄ QUESTION

14   **A) A Carpenter**

Carpenters, with a 37% rate of construction site fatalities, are
hit hardest. (Thought we were going to say nailed, didn't you?)
Electricians are a very close second—just a wire away—at
36%. Roofers—with a good overview of everything—are
at the low end with only 27% of fatal construction-site
accidents. The good news: a total of less than 250 deaths a
year—about the same as farming accidents.

Source: Bureau of Labor Statistics 2002

◄ QUESTION

15   **B) 5 in 7**

In 1962, unable to catch themselves, two fell to their deaths.
The troupe returned to the scene of their catastrophe
(Detroit) in 1998 for another attempt—which they
performed safely 38 times over the following 17 days
proving once and for all that they were more balanced
than most people had thought.

Source: Wallenda.com 2005

◄ QUESTION

16 What Are They Cheering About?

Those peppy, perky, preppy girls in your school's cheerleading pyramid are how much more likely to be seriously injured or killed compared to those peppy, perky female gymnasts?

A) Half as Likely
B) Twice as Likely
C) Three Times as Likely

ANSWER ▶

17 Tan Ban?

It's no secret that overexposure to the sun can cause skin cancer. A 10% increase in exposure will increase your odds of developing a deadly melanoma by how much?

A) 5–9%
B) 12–15%
C) 16–19%

ANSWER ▶

18 Stunning Results—

Tasers—50,000-volt, dart-firing guns—are used by police to avoid deadly force. But over 70 Taser deaths have been recorded. What are the chances that a suspect who died after being "tasered" had been jolted multiple times?

A) 70%
B) 50%
C) 30%

ANSWER ▶

16   C) Three Times as Likely

From 1982 through 1997, 34 female cheerleaders were permanently sidelined by fatal or catastrophic injuries compared to 11 female gymnasts. All in all, the tricks of those two sports are among the riskiest activities for girls—riskier than swimming, track, basketball, field hockey, softball, soccer, lacrosse, volleyball, and downhill skiing combined—maybe even more than sex!

Source: The Physician and Sportsmedicine 1999

◀ Q U E S T I O N

17   C) 16–19%

UV kill me! UV kill me! Repeat this mantra whenever you go out in the sun. Skin cancer is the most common cancer in the U.S. with an average of 1.3 million cases a year. Melanomas—about 4% of all skin cancers—cause *80%* of all skin cancer *deaths* (7,400). Fair-skinned people are particularly susceptible, so limit your exposure to the sun—*especially* if you look like Michael Jackson.

Source: National Cancer Institute 2005

◀ Q U E S T I O N

18   B) 50%

More than half the Taser fatalities involved multiple jolts, easily discharged through the fishhook-like wire and barb by repeated pulls on the trigger. At 50,000 volts, a single 5-second "discharge" of a Taser could run a few large houses for over a year! But voltage is low-amp so, while causing intense pain and instant incapacitation, a single shot would not be deadly. Nor does it leave significant marks. Stunning!

Source: Amnesty International 2005

◀ Q U E S T I O N

Sitting Ducks?

19

For a cop, being shot at is, unfortunately, part of the job description. Taxi drivers don't get combat pay, though maybe they should. What are the on-the-job odds of a murder victim being a taxi driver compared to those of a cop?

A) Half as Likely
B) Equally Likely
C) Twice as Likely

ANSWER ▶

Lumbering On

20

Modern-day Paul Bunyans are still out in the woods among big trees, chain saws, and trucks. Which is most likely to permanently fell a lumberjack?

A) Chain Saw
B) Loading Equipment
C) Falling Object

ANSWER ▶

Disconnect?

21

Steering a moving vehicle with one hand while talking on a cell phone held in the other could give multitasking a bad name. In a car crash, what are the odds it's a woman instead of a man behind the wheel and on the phone?

A) 1 to 1
B) 2 to 1
C) 5 to 1

ANSWER ▶

19   ## A) Half as Likely

The old crime meter is running up quite a tab—about 70 cabbies murdered a year nationwide, compared to about 150 cops (who at least have a shot at shooting back). Add gridlock, "fares" with attitudes, and no-tipping tourists, and it's easy to see why De Niro's character in *Taxi Driver* was so on edge. *Or was it his own checkered past?*

Source: OSHA

◀ QUESTION

20   ## C) Falling Object

Causes of the 991 logging deaths between '92 and '99 were splintered between chain saws (2%), loading equipment (14%), and falling objects like trees, logs, and tree limbs (67%). *Do you think they still yell, "Timber!"?*

Source: Census of Fatal Occupational Injuries, 1992–1999

◀ QUESTION

21   ## B) 2 to 1

Two-thirds (197,000) of all incidents involving cell phones (292,000) are attributed to women drivers. And while the total represents slightly less than 1% of all car crashes, the under-30 crowd contributes 3 times more to that total than any other age group. *It all gives a whole new meaning to the idea of "roll-over minutes."*

Source: National Highway Transportation Safety Association 2002

◀ QUESTION

6

Crime & Punishment

"You can get much farther with a kind word and a gun than you can with a kind word alone."

— AL CAPONE —

What are the odds of getting away with murder? Or not having to serve time for a crime? Is it safer on the street or in your house... during the day or at night? What's the chance of a member of Congress going to jail, or a suspect jumping bail?

From great escapes to the state of executions, it's crime and punishment like you've never seen it before!

Judge for yourself.

Getting Away with Murder—

1

What's the chance that someone will be murdered and no one will be convicted?

A) 1 in 3
B) 1 in 10
C) 1 in 30

ANSWER ▶

Great Escapes?

2

Except for some really lonely guys, it's safe to say that most prisoners would like to get out. What's the chance that a state prison inmate will escape and *not* be quickly returned?

A) 1 in 2,800
B) 1 in 5,600
C) 1 in 8,400

ANSWER ▶

Corporate Lie-abilities

3

When it came to inflating profits and cooking the books, the heads of companies like Enron, Tyco, and WorldCom were good! What's the chance that an exec charged by the CFT has been convicted of fraud or pleaded guilty?

A) 25%
B) 55%
C) 85%

ANSWER ▶

1

A) 1 in 3

Pretty chilling if you're into "closure" or the hope that being caught is a deterrent to crime. Murder has one of the highest "clearance rates" of *any* crime, but it has fallen from a 1965 high of 91% to a 2002 low of 64%. Of the 17,000 *annual* homicides in the U.S., over 5,000 perpetrators are left unknown or unconvictable—beyond a shadow of a doubt. *So it wasn't only O.J.*

Source: FBI 1997

◀ Q U E S T I O N

2

B) 1 in 5,600

In 1998, out of a total state prison population of 1.1 million, a little over 6,500 inmates escaped, but over 97% were quickly recaptured. This, of course, left about 195 "at large" but did alleviate some of the overcrowding in prisons and provided ongoing material for *America's Most Wanted*.

Source: Bureau of Prisons 1998

◀ Q U E S T I O N

3

B) 55%

The Corporate Fraud Task Force has 500 convictions and guilty pleas from 900 defendants, beginning the parade of guys like Bernie Ebbers, Andrew Fastow, and Dennis Kozlowski out from under their corporate umbrellas and golden parachutes, into more suitable prison garb. Facing jail time, fines, and legal fees in the tens of millions, there may be justice after all.

Source: NYTimes 2005

◀ Q U E S T I O N

Fed-Exing—

4

The "feds" have a permanent solution to serious crime. Of the 37 prisoners executed in federal prisons since the practice began in 1927, what are the chances that the crime is murder?

A) 29%
B) 59%
C) 89%

A N S W E R ▶

The State of Execution—

5

Texas is second to California in the number of inmates on death row but leads the country in executions. Of inmates awaiting execution in Texas, the chances are 2 in 25 an inmate will be done in by which of the following fates?

A) Murder
B) Suicide
C) Natural Causes

A N S W E R ▶

Iranians Getting Stoned—

6

While people lose their heads over offenses in Iran, it seems nothing gets a mullah madder than adultery. What are the odds of a woman, compared to a man, being stoned to death for adultery?

A) 1 to 2
B) 1 to 1
C) 2 to 1

A N S W E R ▶

4 **B) 59%**

Only 22 of the prisoners executed had been convicted of murder. The other crimes were bank robbery, sabotage, espionage, and kidnapping. Of the executions, 8 were hanged, 6 got the gas chamber, and 13 got "The Chair." The "big jab" (lethal injection) was first used in 2001 to put away Timothy McVeigh for the 1995 bombing in Oklahoma City, which killed 168.

Source: Amnesty International

◀ Q U E S T I O N

5 **C) Natural Causes**

Efficient as Texans may think they are, they clearly can't kill these folks fast enough. While awaiting execution there have been 17 natural deaths, 5 suicides, 3 murders, and— in the "excuse the mistake" category—5 acquittals, and other reversals.

Source: deathpenalty.org 2005

◀ Q U E S T I O N

6 **C) 2 to 1**

When you've got a 12th-century mindset (and some large stones), this must be how you get your rocks off. This enlightened practice has resulted in 25 stoning sentences, 17 of which were carried out against women, 8 against men. Kinda makes you wonder why there were only 8…

Source: Amnesty International 2005

◀ Q U E S T I O N

Barring Elected Officials—

7 Of the 27 elected officials in the U.S. imprisoned for bribery, fraud, and other felonies, the chances are about 80% that the wrongdoers served in which of the following capacities?

A) U.S. Representatives
B) U.S. Senators
C) State Governors

ANSWER ▶

Comeback Kids?

8 A released prisoner is likeliest to be re-arrested within three years if the first crime was in which of the following categories?

Return to Sender!

A) Drug Offenses
B) Property Crimes
C) Violent Crimes

ANSWER ▶

Do the Crime, Skip the Time—

9 Most felons get away with their crimes—either because they weren't prosecuted or were never arrested. If you're *convicted* of a felony in a U.S. state court, what are the chances that you *won't serve* any jail or prison time?

A) 1 in 10
B) 3 in 10
C) 5 in 10

ANSWER ▶

7 A) U.S. Representatives

From lawmakers to lawbreakers—among the best elected officials money could buy. But perhaps not the brightest, or they'd have been clever enough *(as some have been)* to make their crime legal. The luckiest of this group got to do their time at "Club Fed," Fort Walton Beach, Florida, where inmates once could wear their own clothes and even go home for dinner with their families!

Source: Constitution.org

◄ Q U E S T I O N

8 B) Property Crimes

Stealing—more often than not from the elderly—is one of the easiest crimes to commit and has the highest rearrest rate of the three offenses. About half of all former convicts will be rearrested within three years of being released. Of those, 21% will be convicted and again sent to prison. No wonder jails and prisons are no longer referred to as "correctional institutions."

Source: NWIHC; ABCNews.com 2003

◄ Q U E S T I O N

9 B) 3 in 10

Other than time waiting for trial, about 32% of convicted felons are sentenced to straight probation with no further detention at all. Fortunately for us unsuspecting citizens, most of these probationers are nonviolent. In fact, only about a quarter of them are murderers, rapists, and robbers—*and that's of the 64% they were able to convict!*

Source: Bureau of Justice Statistics

◄ Q U E S T I O N

Night and Day—

10   "Under cover of darkness" has always had sinister implications. After all, even Cinderella had to be home by midnight. What are the odds of a violent crime being committed during the day, between 6 a.m. and 6 p.m.?

A) 1 to 5
B) 1 to 2
C) 1 to 1

A N S W E R ▶

Sex Matters—

11   Of the current U.S. population, what's the chance that a murder victim will be a white female?

XX-Factor!

A) 1 in 10
B) 1 in 30
C) 1 in 50

A N S W E R ▶

Crime Has Its Place—

12   Of the following places, where are you most likely to be a victim of violent crime?

A) At Home
B) Streets Away from Home
C) A Commercial Site

A N S W E R ▶

10 **C) 1 to 1**

Even odds. So much for the shadowy figures behind every bush. Although two-thirds of rapes do happen at night, overall, more than half of other violent crimes are committed during daylight hours. If you have a pit bull, consider making him (or her) a permanent part of your entourage—day and night.

Source: Department of Justice 2003

◀ Q U E S T I O N

11 **C) 1 in 50**

TV crime dramas notwithstanding, it's pretty good to be white, bright, and female. As the largest population group in the country, white females account for only 2% of all homicides. The rate is about 5 times higher for black females and 3 times higher for Hispanics. But no matter what your skin type, your odds are dramatically worse if your significant other is the jealous type.

Source: U.S. Department of Justice 2004

◀ Q U E S T I O N

12 **A) At Home**

One in four violent crimes occurs at or in the home, 17% on streets other than those near the home. With only 7% at commercial establishments, you're safer shopping than you are taking a walk around your block. But then a stranger isn't as likely to beat you up as someone you know or love.

Source: Department of Justice 2003

◀ Q U E S T I O N

Gray Matter—

13

The jails are full of young punks who'd kill you for a dime bag of crack. What's the chance of there being a recently incarcerated, over-55 "Pops" figure among them?

A) 1 in 20
B) 1 in 6
C) 1 in 4

ANSWER ▶

High Jumpers?

14

What's the chance that a suspect released on bail will simply take a hike?

Premature Evacuation!

A) 1 in 4
B) 1 in 10
C) 1 in 25

ANSWER ▶

Turnabout Is Fair Prey?

15

Recidivism rates in the U.S. for sexual predators range between 60% and 80%. What are the chances that a convicted rapist or other sex offender is on parole or probation?

A) 3 in 9
B) 3 in 6
C) 3 in 4

ANSWER ▶

13 **C) 1 in 4**

Kind of a midlife crisis for a "made man" to be sent up the river when most of his peers have stopped rowing altogether. But that, we suppose, is part of the thrill of the crime biz— king of the underworld one day, a prison plaything the next.

Source: Bureau of Prisons 2005

◄ Q U E S T I O N

14 **A) 1 in 4**

In 1997 alone, 33,000 prisoners out on bail nationwide skipped their court hearings and headed out of town. Bounty hunters (or "recovery agents," as they like to be called) brought back about 88%; and the police got another 10%. But that left over 600 at large and looking for life support, possibly at a convenience store near you.

Source: Bureau of Justice Statistics 2002

◄ Q U E S T I O N

15 **C) 3 in 4**

For every convicted sex offender in prison, 3 are out on probation or parole. Of the 60% or more who will be arrested for sex offenses again, approximately 25% will be convicted. Maybe when these predatory perverts are caught they should have their "weapons" removed before being released a second time.

Source: Bureau of Justice Statistics 2005

◄ Q U E S T I O N

Rock Stars—

16   Alcatraz, the maximum-security prison in San Francisco Bay, once housed the country's most violent criminals. Of the 36 inmates who attempted to break out of "The Rock,"

what were
their odds of
succeeding?

A) 6 to 1
B) 3 to 1
C) Zero

ANSWER ▶

A Minimum of Security?

17   U.S. prisons house about 25% of the world's prison population. Chances are that you'll find about 11% of these inmates confined in which level of prison security?

A) Low/Minimum
B) Medium
C) High/Maximum

ANSWER ▶

Foreign Imports?

18   Excluding Guantanamo Bay, there are 182,000 prisoners in U.S. penitentiaries. What are the chances that any one of them is *not* a U.S. citizen?

A) 3 in 10
B) 3 in 100
C) 3 in 1,000

ANSWER ▶

16   A) 6 to 1

Home to such notables as Al Capone, "Birdman" Robert Stroud, and Machine Gun Kelly, Alcatraz, in its 29 years as the country's premier "No Exit" federal pen, had 14 escape attempts involving 36 inmates: 22 were caught and returned; 7 were shot and killed; and 2 drowned. Five listed as "never found" were presumed to have perished in the cold, turbulent, shark-infested waters surrounding The Rock.

Source: The National Park Service 2005

◀ Q U E S T I O N

17   C) High/Maximum

The razor wire and cement toilets of maximum security are for the worst of the worst 11%. Another 25% are housed in medium-security digs. The really well-behaved and white-collar perps (around 60%) can stroll minimum-security grounds, do some networking—with the chance of meeting politicians, occasional celebs, or domestic divas—and start planning partnerships for their futures on the outside.

Source: Bureau of Prisons 2005

◀ Q U E S T I O N

18   A) 3 in 10

Want to be a federal prison guard—*and how many of our avid readers don't?*—you'd better learn to *habla Español*. Almost 30% of all federal prisoners are *not* U.S. citizens—two-thirds of them from neighbors to the south. Most (31,000) are from Mexico, with about 7,000 more from the Dominican Republic and Colombia, and 2,000 from Cuba. Amazingly, the majority drove across the border *in the same car.*

Source: Federal Bureau of Prisons

◀ Q U E S T I O N

Girls in Residence—

19
If you're a young guy looking for a lot of savvy girls who apparently like living life on the edge, in which of the following states would you most likely to find the darlings of your dreams?

A) Wyoming
B) New Jersey
C) Texas

ANSWER ▶

My Little Runaway—

20
In the U.S., a juvenile arrested for being a runaway is most likely to be which of the following?

A Future
Record Holder!

A) A Boy
B) A Girl
C) Named Huckleberry

ANSWER ▶

Proposition X—

21
Prostitution is illegal everywhere in the U.S. except 10 counties in Nevada, including the infamous Mustang Ranch. If you're the "john" and you're not in Nevada, what are the chances of being arrested for soliciting sex?

A) 3%
B) 10%
C) 30%

ANSWER ▶

19   A) Wyoming

Yippy tie-o ki-a! For reasons that remain unclear, the heartland excels at breeding budding Bonnie Parkers. Wyoming is number one, with 40% of its juvenile homes filled with girls. New Jersey has nearly 15%, and Texas has 10%. Nationwide, juvenile girls represent 1 in every 7 in "residential" placements. *Too bad Martha was stuck in West Virginia. She might have mentored some of them into moguls.*

Source: Juvenile Offenders and Victims: 1999 National Report

◀ Q U E S T I O N

20   B) A Girl

Girls comprise about 60% of all runaway arrests, though there's no telling whether that's because boys can simply run faster or they have no place to go. Which is why Huck Finn won't ever be arrested—and the reason he lit out for Indian territory in the first place.

Source: Center on Juvenile and Criminal Justice

◀ Q U E S T I O N

21   B) 10%

Call it entrapment, mistaken identity, or just a lapse in judgment, you're still screwed if you're caught buying sex, whether by your significant other or the police. Legal penalties range from fines and probation to fines and a night or two in jail. But at 1 to 9 odds, you're probably home free. Penalties from your live-in love, however, could be far more painful, *and longer lasting.*

Source: National Taskforce on Prostitution 1998

◀ Q U E S T I O N

140

Purloined Persona—

22   If you've been a victim of identity theft, you're not alone. According to the FTC, there are about 3 million victims a year in the U.S. What's the chance the thief is someone you know?

A) 1 to 1
B) 10 to 1
C) 100 to 1

ANSWER ▶

Drug Seizures—

23   Hmm…whether to toot, tar, or toke? A pound of illegal drugs seized by the federal government is likeliest to be which of the following?

A) Cocaine
B) Heroin
C) Marijuana

ANSWER ▶

Spectator Sport?

24   Soccer is huge in Latin America, but kidnapping has also become something of a national pastime. Of the worldwide kidnappings in 1999, what were the odds of someone being snatched in Latin America?

A) 3 to 1
B) 5 to 1
C) 9 to 1

ANSWER ▶

22 **A) 1 to 1**

Who can you trust? A recent study by Visa concluded that
over half of all identity thefts were perpetrated by a family
member, friend, or employee. So watch your back—and your
receipts—at family reunions, backyard barbecues, and those
office Christmas parties. And remember, as you're thinking
of turning one of them in, these folks would also be *the most
likely suspects* if you were to be murdered.

Source: The New York Times 2005

◀ Q U E S T I O N

23 **C) Marijuana**

The feds seized 2.9 million pounds of drugs in 2001—
245,000 pounds of coke, 5,500 pounds of H, and a whopping
2.67 million pounds of good old Mary Jane. No telling what
kind of economic impact this has had on the snack-food
industry.

Source: U.S. Statistical Abstract

◀ Q U E S T I O N

24 **C) 9 to 1**

Over 90% of kidnappings worldwide in 1999 were in Central
or South America. Colombia led the pack with 972, followed
by Mexico (402), Brazil (51), Ecuador (12), and Venezuela
(12). Between '92 and '99, 7,050 of the 7,773 kidnappings—of
children and adults for ransom—were in these countries. *If
you work for a high-profile U.S. company, you might want to skip
junkets to these regions.*

Source: FBI National Crime Information Center 2001

◀ Q U E S T I O N

Elementary, My Dear Watson?

25 Juvenile boys who had committed an assault by the time they were 16 were most likely to have already done which of the following by age 12?

A) Destroyed Property
B) Sold Drugs
C) Carried a Handgun

ANSWER ▶

Shots in the Dark—

26 In the U.S., what's the chance that a firearm transfer application will be rejected based on a background check?

You Fill in the Blanks!

A) 1 in 45
B) 1 in 25
C) 1 in 5

ANSWER ▶

Come On, Baby, Light My Fire—

27 About 180 people a year are killed as a result of arson. What's the chance that a suspected arsonist is under age 18?

A) Less than 20%
B) 20 to 40%
C) Over 40%

ANSWER ▶

25   A) Destroyed Property

It shouldn't take a Sherlock Holmes to see this coming: by age 12, 79% had already purposely destroyed property, 63% had committed an assault, and 60% had carried a concealed handgun. Over half belonged to a gang, 21% had been arrested before, and 10% had sold drugs. As for personal habits, 39% smoked and 31% drank. *(For a five-point bonus, guess the number of these kids who were planned progeny.)*

Source: Juvenile Offenders and Victims: 1999 National Report

◀ Q U E S T I O N

26   A) 1 in 45

Since the inception of the Brady Act, 38 million firearm transfer applications have been checked, but only 840,000 have been rejected. Over half of the rejections were due to prior felony convictions—*forcing 420,000 felons to obtain their weapons illegally!*

Source: Bureau of Justice Statistics

◀ Q U E S T I O N

27   C) Over 40%

To quote Beavis, *"Fire! Fire!"* Juveniles account for nearly half of all arson arrests. On the positive side, at least they're goal-oriented and using matches for a reason—*not just playing with them.*

Source: FBI; DSM-IV-TR

◀ Q U E S T I O N

144

Do Unto Others?

28 In 2003 in the U.S., there were 9,100 victims of hate crimes. Of the following groups, which was the most likely to be targeted?

A) Blacks
B) Homosexuals
C) Muslims

ANSWER ▶

Hey, Dude, That's My Car!

29 During 2003, a vehicle stolen in the U.S. was most likely which of the following models?

Highway Robbery!

A) 1995 Saturn SL
B) 1998 Acura Integra
C) 1991 Ferrari

ANSWER ▶

Please Don't Show Us Your Briefs—

30 What's the chance that the U.S. Supreme Court will actually choose to rule on any given petition officially submitted to it?

A) 1 in 900
B) 1 in 90
C) 1 in 9

ANSWER ▶

28   **A) Blacks**

In 2003 there were still far more hate crimes against blacks (51%) than any other group. Hate crimes against homosexuals accounted for 17%, and those against Muslims accounted for 11%. Other religious groups were also targeted, including atheists, who were apparently targeted for their *disbeliefs*.

Source: FBI Hate Crime Statistics 2003

◀ Q U E S T I O N

29   **A) 1995 Saturn SL**

The '95 Saturn SL was the top choice of auto thieves in 2003. But both Saturns and Acuras are very popular, probably because of the value of their parts. In fact, 6 of the top 25 stolen-car models were Acuras which use similar components year to year. Ferraris, however, haven't been stolen regularly since the third season of *Miami Vice*.

Source: CCC Information Services 2005

◀ Q U E S T I O N

30   **B) 1 in 90**

Each term, about 7,000 cases are officially submitted to the U.S. Supreme Court, but the justices rule on only about 80 per term. So, if someone threatens to take you all the way to the Supreme Court, not to worry—unless your opponent has "deep pockets." Deep pockets probably still won't get either of you to the Supreme Court, but they certainly can take you to the cleaners.

Source: Washington Post 1999

◀ Q U E S T I O N

Politics & World Events

66 Perhaps in time the so-called Dark Ages
will be thought of as including our own. 99
— G.C. LICHTENBERG (1742–1799) —

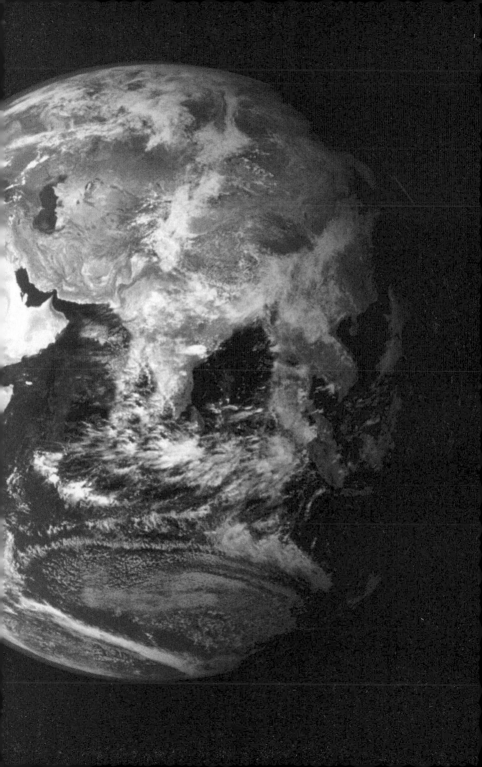

Step up to the world stage and test your odds IQ on events current and historical. From the U.S. Civil War to Napoleon's retreat from Moscow, to the current conflict in Iraq; from FMG—what it is and where it's practiced—to evolution "theory" and the American presidency. Odds amazing, baffling, and bizarre—just like the real world.

Come on, people, the world awaits!

Survival of the Witless?

1   What are the chances that a U.S. state currently has a law challenging the validity of evolution "theory"?

A) 3 in 50
B) 11 in 50
C) 17 in 50

ANSWER ▶

Rites and Wrongs—

2   FMG, female genital mutilation, is performed on an estimated 6,000 girls and women every day throughout the world. In which country is a girl most likely to undergo some form of this torturous practice?

A) Egypt
B) Ghana
C) Uganda

ANSWER ▶

Napoleonic Plague—

3   On the five-month march to invade Russia in 1812, what were the chances of Napoleon's troops dying from disease, even before the battles began?

A) 10%
B) 20%
C) 40%

ANSWER ▶

1   **C) 17 in 50**

Let Darwin, Darrow, and Galileo burn in hell! So sayeth
voters in the 17 states out to thwart the teaching of the
science of evolution with a variety of tactics, including
warning labels in high school biology books. Strangely, no
compromise is in the works to label both evolution *and*
the Bible as "theories" or agree on the possibility that God
rested on the "seventh day" to let things *evolve*.

Source: MSNBC.com; Tolerance.org

◀ Q U E S T I O N

2   **A) Egypt**

The legacy of the Pharaohs is alive and well in Egypt, where
an estimated 97% of girls continue to undergo FMG. Ghana
(15–30%) and Uganda (5%) are 2 of more than 25 African
countries in which FMG is still practiced. Efforts to eradicate
FMG have had negligible effects. We wonder how long such a
practice would have lasted if men in these countries had to
put their privates on the chopper.

Source: Amnesty International 2005

◀ Q U E S T I O N

3   **C) 40%**

Between dysentery, diarrhea, and an array of other ailments,
over a third of Napoleon's 500,000 troops ended up with
lives as short as their leader. And that was before the
fighting started! When they finally reached Moscow, the
Russians had already razed it to the ground. All in all, only
20,000 of the original half-million troops survived.

Source: Encyclopedia of Plague & Pestilence, G.C. Kohn, ed.

◀ Q U E S T I O N

Staying Power—

4   While today's war in Iraq is a relatively small conflict compared to previous wars the U.S. has fought, what are the odds that a U.S. soldier wounded in Iraq will survive a hit, compared to a soldier in WWII?

A) 4 to 3
B) 4 to 2
C) 4 to 1

ANSWER ▶

Men About the House—

5   In which country is a member of the national parliament *least* likely to be female?

Parliamentary Procedure!

A) France
B) Sweden
C) England

ANSWER ▶

Tanks for Nothing

6   Which of the following countries is most likely to spend the *least* on its military this year?

A) Germany
B) Japan
C) Israel

ANSWER ▶

4   A) 4 to 3

God bless America! And its medical and tactical advances, all of which have increased the likelihood of soldier survival from 67% in WWII to 75% in Vietnam to about 90% in the current conflict in Iraq. Of course, the ironic flipside of these life-saving techniques is the unprecedented number of badly wounded soldiers who need an iron will to adjust to the often severe limitations of their new physical condition.

Source: Army News Service

◄ Q U E S T I O N

5   A) France

Need we remind you which language gave us the word *chauvinist*? With a scant 12% female representation, France is at the back of the pack. The Brits, at 18%, are only slightly ahead of the French. Congrats go to the Swedes whose legislative body is a whopping 45% female! Do they do massages, too?

Source: The Social Situation in the European Union *2003*

◄ Q U E S T I O N

6   C) Israel

Despite its reputation for being armed to the hilt, Israel's $10 billion in annual military expenditures is far outweighed by Germany's $27.2 billion and Japan's $47 billion—the second-largest military budget in the world after the U.S. Is it just us, or didn't the militarization of Germany and Japan cause us problems in the past? *Hmmm...*

Source: Stockholm Int'l Peace Research Institute

◄ Q U E S T I O N

General-Lee Speaking—

7 What were the odds of becoming one of the troop casualties suffered under the direct command of Robert E. Lee, compared to those of his opponents in battle?

A) 3 to 1
B) Even Odds
C) 1 to 3

ANSWER ▶

White was Might—

8 Of the estimated 650,000 Native Americans who died from unnatural causes in the 19th century, what was the chance of an individual being killed in battle?

A) 1 in 100
B) 1 in 50
C) 1 in 10

ANSWER ▶

Free to Be—

9 What are the chances that anyone living on earth today lives in a democratic nation?

A) 17 in 100
B) 37 in 100
C) 57 in 100

ANSWER ▶

7   **A) 3 to 1**

Despite his military brilliance, Lee still lost a higher percentage of his men (over 20%) than the Union forces arrayed against him. But Lee's losses (11%) were nowhere near the 50% casualty rate sustained under the command of fellow Confederate general, J.C. Pemberton—*which is probably why the Dukes of Hazzard didn't name their car after him.*

Source: Attack and Die McWhinney & Jamieson

◀ QUESTION

8   **C) 1 in 10**

Approximately 65,000 Native Americans actually died in the 1800s as a result of armed conflicts with settlers and the U.S. army. The majority of the other untimely deaths were the result of European diseases and starvation. But, in the "turnabout is fair play" category, Indian casinos are now scalping more white men than Sitting Bull ever dreamed of!

Source: users.erols.com

◀ QUESTION

9   **C) 57 in 100**

Buoyed by India's huge electorate of over a billion, the majority of people worldwide can now claim to live in some form of democratic society. But before we break out into paroxysms of democratic self-congratulation, let's remember that there are still some 3 billion people in the world disenfranchised, save for their local version of *American Idol.*

Source: UN Human Development Report

◀ QUESTION

No, Canada—

10 What are the chances that an American has a "somewhat unfavorable" or "very unfavorable" opinion of Canada?

A) 25%
B) 50%
C) 75%

ANSWER ▶

Value Added—

11 As of 2001, what were the chances that a current U.S. senator was a millionaire?

The Buck Stops Here!

A) 1 in 5
B) 2 in 5
C) 3 in 5

ANSWER ▶

A Show of Hands—

12 In which of the following countries are you *most* likely to have to bribe a government official to get things done?

A) Colombia
B) Turkey
C) Finland

ANSWER ▶

10   **A) 25%**

What the hey, eh? Nearly a quarter of Americans don't think much of our neighbors to the north, and you can bet that Canadians aren't thrilled about constantly being characterized as our 51st state. Come on, people! Can't we put this whole French and Indian War thing behind us?

Source: Pew Research Center 2004

◀ Q U E S T I O N

11   **B) 2 in 5**

Of 100 U.S. senators, 40 qualified as millionaires, and 2 (John Kerry and Herb Kohl) have fortunes worth over $100 million each. On the other hand, only 10% of U.S. senators report a net worth of less than $100,000. And let's stress that word "report."

Source: CNN.com 2003

◀ Q U E S T I O N

12   **B) Turkey**

Turkey ranks 77th on the world's corruption index, below the drug-fueled economy of Colombia (59th) and well back of the not-so-perfect U.S. (18th)—all ahead of Haiti and Bangladesh, tied for last at 145th. But you'll never have to slip a Finn a fin: Finland is the earth's least corrupt nation—or maybe that's just what they've conned the TICP into thinking!

Source: Transparency International Corruption Perceptions Index 2004

◀ Q U E S T I O N

The Bachelor Party?

13 What are the chances that a president of the United States never married?

A) 2 in 42
B) 1 in 42
C) Zero

ANSWER ▶

Collateral Damage—

14 What were the odds that a death attributable to WWII's European and Pacific campaigns was that of a civilian?

A) 5 to 1
B) 3 to 1
C) 2 to 1

ANSWER ▶

This Land is Whose Land?

15 What are the chances that a piece of land in the 50 United States is owned by the federal government?

A) 3 in 100
B) 3 in 10
C) 3 in 5

ANSWER ▶

13   **B) 1 in 42**

With the sole exception of lifelong bachelor James Buchanan (1791–1868), all 42 U.S. presidents had been married at least once by the time they assumed office. As for why James B. remained a bachelor, only his hairdresser knows for sure.

Source: WhiteHouse.gov

◀ Q U E S T I O N

14   **C) 2 to 1**

Sixty-seven percent of all deaths in WWII were of civilians. No wonder so many of our enemies (over 12%) joined the military—maybe it was the *safest* place to be.

Source: World-War-2.info

◀ Q U E S T I O N

15   **B) 3 in 10**

Uncle Sam actually owns about 31% of all the land in the U.S., including over 85% of Nevada, the state with the highest proportion of federally owned land. Word has it that the rest of Nevada is owned by "the house."

Source: National Wilderness Institute 2004

◀ Q U E S T I O N

Neighborhood Watch?

16 What are the chances that an American favors legislation allowing the CIA to spy *inside* the U.S.?

A) Over 20%
B) Over 40%
C) Over 60%

ANSWER ▶

White Anglo-Saxon Presidents—

17 So far, the spectrum of U.S. presidents has ranged from white to white, male to male, and one form of Christianity to another. Of the following denominations, which has been most likely to provide any given U.S. president?

A) Methodist
B) Presbyterian
C) Episcopalian

ANSWER ▶

Background Check—

18 If you want to become leader of the free world as president of the U.S., you have the *worst* odds of success with which of the following jobs on your résumé?

A) State Governor
B) U.S. Senator
C) U.S. Representative

ANSWER ▶

16 **C) Over 60%**

The majority of Americans would have no problem with the Agency conducting operations "in house," as it were. And why not? It isn't like the CIA has ever abused its power overseas. Why would they do it here?

Source: Time; CNN

◀ Q U E S T I O N

17 **C) Episcopalian**

The Episcopal Church has been the church of choice for 11 presidents. Six Presbyterians have become top dog, as have 5 Methodists. With the election of JFK, the Catholic barrier was broken, and though it didn't work for John Kerry, it does leave room for lots of other sects praying for their man, woman—or something in between.

Source: WhiteHouse.gov

◀ Q U E S T I O N

18 **B) U.S. Senator**

With 19 presidents each, it appears that heading the state house or serving in the House of Representatives is the surest route to the U.S. presidency. A career in the Senate— with all those impossible-to-explain votes—can be a candidate's ball and chain in today's media-sound-byte society. Just ask John Kerry and Bob Dole. *Actually, on second thought, don't.*

Source: WhiteHouse.gov

◀ Q U E S T I O N

A Two-for-One Deal—

19 Not every pairing of U.S. presidents and vice presidents was made in heaven. What are the chances that a president has had more than one vice president during his term(s) in office?

A) 5%
B) 15%
C) 20%

ANSWER ▶

Oh-So-Soft—

20 Since 1989, which organization has been the *second* largest donor to U.S. political races?

The Gift Horse!

A) AMA (Doctors)
B) NEA (Teachers)
C) RJR (Suits, Smoking)

ANSWER ▶

Vanishing Acts—

21 Valor and bravery were major parts of the Civil War, but so was desertion. Of all desertions during the conflict, what were the odds that any given one was from the Union compared to the Confederate side?

A) 1 to 2
B) Even Odds
C) 2 to 1

ANSWER ▶

19 ## C) 20%

Eight of our former presidents changed sidekicks during
their term(s)—Jefferson, Madison, Lincoln, Grant, McKinley,
Franklin Roosevelt, and Nixon. In fact, FDR had *three*
separate vice presidents, a rate of rotation that made
his administration sort of the Destiny's Child of
American history.

Source: WhiteHouse.gov

◀ QUESTION

20 ## B) NEA (Teachers)

So—just how many teachers *can* sleep in the Lincoln
bedroom at one time? But, of course, there's a lesson here.
This teachers union outspends doctors, teamsters, and pretty
much everyone else except the #1 donor—the American
Federation of State, County, and Municipal Employees. Just
remember that the next time you think
you can bribe *any of them* with a measly apple.

Source: OpenSecrets.org 2003

◀ QUESTION

21 ## C) 2 to 1

More than twice as many Union troops deserted (188,000)
as Confederates (83,400). And, while the North's total force
of 2.5 million was about twice that of the South's 1.2 million,
the North's desertion rate was still about 20% higher than
the South's. Devotion to the Cause? Protecting home and
hearth? Or Yankee ingenuity: collecting to enlist and serve for
others, often doing so several times? The debate rages on.

Source: The Civil War Centennial Handbook W. Price

◀ QUESTION

Rotten to the Core

22 Since 1996, what are the chances that a U.S. nuclear reactor has been reported for safety violations?

A) 3 in 10
B) 6 in 10
C) 9 in 10

ANSWER ▶

Madam, "I Do!"

23 What's the chance that any particular president of the United States has been sworn into office by a female justice?

On my Honor, Your Honor!

A) Never
B) 1 in 42
C) 2 in 42

ANSWER ▶

Rank Privileges?

24 Compared to the enlisted ranks of soldiers, how likely was it that a British officer would contract polio while fighting in India during WWII?

A) Half as Likely
B) 2 Times as Likely
C) 6 Times as Likely

ANSWER ▶

22 **C) 9 in 10**

Homer Simpson would be proud, but the rest of us have a lot to worry about. A full 91% of U.S. nuclear plants have reported safety violations in the last several years—making us all one big (potentially) dysfunctional nuclear family.

Source: Public Citizen 2004

◀ Q U E S T I O N

23 **B) 1 in 42**

Federal judge Sarah T. Hughes's 1963 swearing-in of Lyndon Johnson was the first and only time a U.S. president was sworn in by a woman—not so surprising, given that it's usually been a Supreme Court justice who administers the oath. And the first woman on the Supreme Court (Sandra Day O'Connor) wasn't appointed until 1981. Heck, women have only been able *to vote* since 1920.

Source: www.whitehouse.gov/history/presidents

◀ Q U E S T I O N

24 **C) 6 Times as Likely**

Though an officer's life was in many ways cushier, the enlisted ranks remained far safer from polio during WWII. Of every 100,000 British officers, 170 contracted the disease, compared to just 30 per 100,000 regulars and 1 in 100,000 locals.

Source: Encyclopedia of Plague & Pestilence G.C. Kohn, ed.

◀ Q U E S T I O N

Hanging Chads?

25 What's the chance that a "red state" that went for Bush in the 2004 election still has an actual gallows for executing convicted murderers?

A) 40%
B) 20%
C) Zero

ANSWER ▶

Playing Second Fiddle—

26 There are few, if any, men who served as U.S. vice presidents who didn't aspire (at least privately) to be the #1 guy. But what are the chances that a VP has done this job for *more* than one president?

A) Zero
B) 1 to 24
C) 2 to 24

ANSWER ▶

<u>Un</u>-Reconstructed—

27 What are the chances that an average Alabama resident voted *to retain* the state's constitutional ban on interracial marriage in the year 2000?

A) 25%
B) 40%
C) 65%

ANSWER ▶

25   C) Zero

While red state Republicans tend to be pro–death penalty, the only legal working gallows are in the blue state of Washington. No word on whether the state also rents them out to law-abiding folks who have simply had enough of the Washington weather.

Source: DeathPenaltyInfo.org

◀ Q U E S T I O N

26   B) 1 in 24

Only two men have been in the position to fiddle around for more than one president: George Clinton (no known relation to Bubba) served as VP to both Jefferson and Madison, while John C. Calhoun served under both John Quincy Adams and Andrew Jackson. Between the two of them, they probably saw more seasons of vice than Crockett and Tubbs.

Source: WhiteHouse.gov

◀ Q U E S T I O N

27   B) 40%

Sweet home, Alabama? Even though the bill lifting the ban on miscegenation did pass, a full 40% of Alabamians still voted in 2000 to preserve it—33 years after the U.S. Supreme Court ruled it unconstitutional! The good news is that it's a 60% improvement.

Source: Alabama Education Association 2003

◀ Q U E S T I O N

The Offensive Line—

28

As the smaller, less-well-armed force in the Civil War, the Confederates were most likely to do which of the following when they took the lead into battle?

A) Get Themselves Killed
B) Inflict Casualties
C) Spit Tobacco

ANSWER ▶

Better Dead Than Red?

29

What are the chances that the average American still thinks a college teacher should be fired for admitting to being a Communist?

A) 7 in 100
B) 17 in 100
C) 37 in 100

ANSWER ▶

Black & White & Unread All Over—

30

A person is most likely to be illiterate in which of the following countries?

A) Nepal
B) Nigeria
C) Norway

ANSWER ▶

28 **A) Get Themselves Killed**

Anyone chewing tobacco could hardly avoid spitting on someone's grave. In over 91% of the battles where the South led the attack, it also took the greatest number of casualties. The worst of these was against Grant at Cold Harbor, where over 45% of the rebels were killed. As defensive fighters, however, the Confederates had a dramatically lower casualty rate than the Union forces.

Source: Attack & Die McWhinney & Jamieson

◀ Q U E S T I O N

29 **C) 37 in 100**

The Red Menace lives! Nearly 40% of Americans still believe that "Commies" have no place in our universities. And to prove it, they've got this blacklist of 205 names...

Source: National Opinion Research Center 2002

◀ Q U E S T I O N

30 **A) Nepal**

Despite its appeal as an exotic tourist destination, Nepal has a literacy rate of only 44%. Nigeria's is 67%. Norway, with a 99% literacy rate, is on top of the world in more than Vikings and fjords.

Source: National Institute for Literacy; UNESCO 2002

◀ Q U E S T I O N

Hopefully You Got
More Politically Correct
Than Incorrect...

Oddities

"I don't want to make the wrong mistake."
—YOGI BERRA —

There's a lot of odd stuff going on out there...

Can you die from flatulence? Who'd rather have a dog than a lover?...And are they mutually exclusive?

Which saints are the busiest?...And how likely are you to roll out of post-op with a foreign object you hadn't bargained for?

See how your odds IQ measures up on Oddities!

Gone with the Wind—

1 What is the chance that anyone in the U.S. will die from flatulence?

A) Zero
B) 1 in 140 Million
C) 1 in 280 Million

ANSWER ▶

Busy Bees—

2 Can you spell M-I-S-S-I-S-S-I-P-P-I? Then pick which of the following states has the best odds of producing a winner in the National Spelling Bee.

A) Indiana
B) Pennsylvania
C) Texas

ANSWER ▶

In the "Ooops" Category—

3 About 200 surgical implements are used in the average operation. What's the chance of someone dying from a "foreign object" mistakenly left in the body during an operation?

A) 1 in 40 Million
B) 9 in 40 Million
C) 19 in 40 Million

ANSWER ▶

1 B) 1 in 140 Million

Whewwww! Who knew? It's hard to imagine, but according to CDC records, between 1999 and 2001 there has been an average of about 2 deaths per year—*from flatulence!* No word on what these unfortunate folks had eaten before they…passed.

Source: CDC 2005

◄ QUESTION

2 C) Texas

The Lone Star State has had the most wins at seven (tied with Colorado); Pennsylvania has had six. Indiana has had zero wins, but it's renowned for the spelling prowess of its native son and former vice president (under Bush I) Dan Quayle. In his bid to impress kids and the media during a classroom campaign stop, Quayle corrected a child's spelling of "potato" by adding an "e" at the end—as in "p-o-t-a-t-o-e."

Source: Encyclopedia Britannica Almanac 2003

◄ QUESTION

3 B) 9 in 40 Million

"We're missing a scalpel!" isn't what you want to hear coming out of post-op. Of the 40 million annual surgeries performed in U.S. hospitals, an average of 9 deaths a year are caused by "foreign objects being left in the body during surgery." *And you thought the* Seinfeld *Junior Mint episode was just a joke!*

Source: CDC 1998

◄ QUESTION

Fantasy Isle, British Style—

4 Of the following top 3 unrealized desires of middle-aged U.K. couples, which *one* are they most likely to fantasize about?

A) Having a Lover
B) Having a Dog
C) Having a Better Body

ANSWER ▶

What's the Connection?

5 The chances are 3 in 5 that "Siamese" or conjoined twins are connected in which of the following ways?

One on One!

A) Facing Each Other
B) Back-to-Back
C) In Another Life

ANSWER ▶

On Comet, on Cupid, on Donald and...Nixon?

6 Clement Moore's *'Twas the Night Before Christmas* is a perennial favorite worldwide. What is the chance that your average American can name all eight of Santa's reindeer from the poem?

A) 5%
B) 25%
C) 45%

ANSWER ▶

4 **B) Having a Dog**

Maybe it's the cuisine, or the weather, but when Brits fantasize, it has a peculiarly English accent. Of course, in a country where one-quarter of couples polled say they're sorry they got married, maybe it's no wonder "having a dog" tops the list of fantasies. And, in the case of Prince Charles, it appears he's managed to combine two of the top three.

Source: Readers Digest (UK) 2001

◀ Q U E S T I O N

5 **A) Facing Each Other**

Live births of conjoined twins only occur once in every 200,000 deliveries. And the greatest number—60% to 65%—are connected at the trunk, facing each other (either Thoracopagus or Omphalopagus); 20% are positioned back-to-back (Pygopagus); only 2% are connected by the tops of their heads (Craniopagus). As for past-life connections, those can only be considered on a séance by séance basis.

Source: Swarthmore.edu; Conjoined Twins International 2005

◀ Q U E S T I O N

6 **B) 25%**

No, Donald and Nixon aren't among the reindeer; nor is Rudolph—he's from the song. In fact, only a quarter of those polled got them all. Ready?... Dasher, Dancer, Prancer, Vixen, Comet, Cupid, Donder, and Blitzen.

Source: Franklin Mills Mall Poll 2002

◀ Q U E S T I O N

S'aint Gonna Happen—

7 In Roman Catholic liturgy, the busiest patron saints are most likely to be those watching over the faithful who find themselves in which of these unfortunate conditions?

A) Depression
B) Demonic Possession
C) Dying Alone

ANSWER ▶

Which End's Up?

8 What is the chance of a baby being born feet or buttocks first?

Special Delivery!

A) 1 in 25
B) 1 in 100
C) 1 in 1,000

ANSWER ▶

Pigging Out—

9 The odds are that the average American will consume approximately how many pounds of pork this year?

A) 20 Pounds
B) 50 Pounds
C) 100 Pounds

ANSWER ▶

7   ## A) Depression

Although there are 9 saints watching over the possessed,
there are a whopping 17 guarding the depressed. Sadly,
only 1—St. Francis of Assisi—guards over those dying
alone…leaving, we suppose, even more work for the 17
anti-depressant saints…

Source: catholic-forum.com 2005

◀ Q U E S T I O N

8   ## A) 1 in 25

Some of those alpha babies are in such a hurry to get out
they don't follow the directions, and 4% present themselves
in a breech position—usually feet or buttocks first. While
breech births were once likely to be fatal to both mother
and child, they're now handled (with good prenatal care)
safely and routinely, usually by cesarean section.

Source: AmericanPregnancy.org

◀ Q U E S T I O N

9   ## B) 50 pounds

Add pickled pigs' feet to those servings of ham, bacon,
sausage, and ribs, and you've got over 50 pounds of pork
consumed by the average American per year—about a pound
a week. No wonder there are so many hog farms with their
attendant—*and noxious*—"lagoons."

Source: U.S. Statistical Abstract 2001

◀ Q U E S T I O N

Spanky and the Gang—

10 State laws prohibiting corporal punishment—spankings and other "physically assertive" measures by teachers on students—were first passed in the 1980s. What's the chance a state still allows corporal punishment?

A) 7 in 50
B) 19 in 50
C) 23 in 50

ANSWER ▶

On Wife Support—

11 Based on past experience, the champion of the World Wife-Carrying Championships is most likely to be from which country?

That's a Load Off My Mind!

A) Estonia
B) Malta
C) Tonga

ANSWER ▶

Believers?

12 Americans are most likely to believe in which of the following?

A) Higher Taxes
B) Handgun Ban
C) The Devil

ANSWER ▶

10 **C) 23 in 50**

Pay attention, kid! Almost half the states—mostly in the South and West—still consider a good smack appropriate punishment. And Texas leads the nation in the number of kids smacked (74,000) and in the number of convicted murderers whacked (338 executions). Something for you kids to consider if Mom and Dad are planning a move.

Source: Federal Education Department, Center for Effective Discipline 2005

◄ Q U E S T I O N

11 **A) Estonia**

Over in the Baltics, they carry you across the threshold and just keep going. An Estonian has won the esteemed World Wife-Carrying Championships the last seven years running. As for how the gals reciprocate, we hear the winners are doing some very uplifting things, whereas the losers are just holding out.

Source: CNN

◄ Q U E S T I O N

12 **C) The Devil**

While only 32% support a handgun ban and a mere 1% support higher taxes, 45% of Americans believe in Beelzebub. In Britain, on the other hand, 83% are opposed to handguns, 62% are for higher taxes, and only 13% say they believe in the devil. *No wonder the Pilgrims left.*

Source; The Economist 2002

◄ Q U E S T I O N

Doesn't Ring a Bell—

13 What are the chances that anyone alive today has *never* made a telephone call?

A) 2 in 3
B) 2 in 300
C) 2 in 3,000

ANSWER ▶

Dino-sorcery—

14 What's the chance that an American believes it's okay to use cloning to reintroduce extinct species?

Redo The Dodo?

A) 1 in 50
B) 1 in 15
C) 1 in 5

ANSWER ▶

Old Before Their Time—

15 Progeria syndrome is a rare genetic disorder that makes very young boys and girls look and feel like little old men and women. What's the chance that if you have one child with this problem, you'll have another?

A) 1 in 500
B) 1 in 5,000
C) 1 in 1,000,000

ANSWER ▶

13   **A) 2 in 3**

No, it's not instant messaging. Hard as it may be for us
21st-century residents of the developed world to believe,
two-thirds of our fellow global citizens haven't even caught
up to the technology of the 20th.

Source: FCC

◀ Q U E S T I O N

14   **C) 1 in 5**

If you see your neighbor walking their velociraptor, you'll
know why. Twenty percent of Americans have no problem
with the notion of regenerating extinct species from DNA.
Must be the same 20% who never saw *Jurassic Park*.

Source: Fox News 2003

◀ Q U E S T I O N

15   **A) 1 in 500**

A second progeria baby born to the same parents would
be rare but still over 10,000 times more likely than in the
general population. This devastating disorder causes stunted
growth, baldness, wrinkling of the skin, delayed tooth
formation, thin limbs, and a life-span that rarely exceeds 27.
A great deal of research is being done on gene therapy which
seems to offer the likeliest route to a cure.
Source: City Hospital NHS Trust, Birmingham, UK

◀ Q U E S T I O N

184

Map Quest, Anyone?

16

What's the chance that an American fourth grader can't identify his or her state on an unmarked U.S. map?

A) 1 in 3
B) 1 in 5
C) 1 in 7

ANSWER ▶

Turkeys, Crows & Starlings Need Not Apply—

17

Add vultures to that group of feathered friends not showing up on the list of state birds. Of the following birds which is most likely to be a "bird-of-state"?

A) Bluebird
B) Mockingbird
C) Cardinal

ANSWER ▶

Hairy Black Tongue—

18

There's not a lot you can add to that distasteful medical description other than I'd never want it in my mouth. You're most likely to contract this disorder from which of the following?

A) Oral Sex
B) Mouthwash
C) Smoking

ANSWER ▶

16   **A) 1 in 3**

A state of ignorance was home to a third of fourth graders who couldn't identify their home states. Even when asked to name the state in which they lived, many named adjacent states or their cities. So, moms and dads, you may want to consider getting those kids a tracking device or sewing their home number into their clothes—*in case they lose their cell phones!*

Source: CBS News 2002

◀ QUESTION

17   **C) Cardinal**

Red birds top the list of chosen state "reps" most often with 7, followed by mockingbirds with 5 and bluebirds with 2. Other states, like Maryland and its Baltimore oriole, chose uniquely indigenous birds. Then there's Minnesota, making a statement—though we're not sure what kind—with the selection of the *common loon.*

Source: 50states.com

◀ QUESTION

18   **C) Smoking**

If the smell of cigarette smoke in your hair and clothes, and the omnipresent threat of cancer and heart disease don't give you pause, think about French-kissing anyone with a HAIRY... BLACK...TONGUE! (Choosing "Mouthwash" merits half a point as it can be caused by the overuse of such products.) There's no established link to oral sex, so you don't have that to worry about, just AIDS and a long list of nasty STDs.

Source: Medline Encyclopedia 2005

◀ QUESTION

What's Really Odd...The Pages with Answers!

Art & Pop Culture

Can art really affect a city's economy?...What are the odds of Shakespeare writing a comedy?... Of a comedy winning an Oscar?... Or of <u>anyone</u>, for that matter, winning an Oscar?

Who's renting what... reading what...and where would you end up in Dante's Inferno?

Grab some popcorn and test your pop-culture IQ.

A Banner Year—

1 For 16 days in February 2005, New York City's Central Park was the staging ground for the conceptual artist Christo's "The Gates." How did the odds of increased visits to the park compare to the norm?

A) 200% Increase
B) 400% Increase
C) 800% Increase

ANSWER ▶

Hot Properties—

2 Which of these blockbuster toy phenomena has *defied* the odds and sold continuously for over twenty years?

Strictly Child's Play!

A) Care Bears
B) Cabbage Patch Kids
C) Furbies

ANSWER ▶

Going Down?

3 In Dante's *Inferno*, if you are in the ninth and lowest circle of hell, odds are that it's because you committed which crime?

A) Blasphemy
B) Treason
C) Dying Unbaptized

ANSWER ▶

1   **B) 400% Increase**

Normal visits to Central Park for the period would
have numbered about 750,000. The $23 million "Gates"
installation (paid for completely by the artist) brought 4
million people to the site—a much larger number of fans
than the Yankees see in an *entire* season. "The Gates" also
generated an estimated $254 million in economic activity for
the city. *And no, it didn't look like anybody's shower curtain.*

Source: NYC Board of Tourism 2005

◀ Q U E S T I O N

2   **B) Cabbage Patch Kids**

Despite predictions that the appeal of those homely kids
would fade after the first riotous year in 1983, they've gone
on to sell over $5 *billion* in dolls and other merchandise.
Care Bears, another '80s phenom was successfully revived in
2002, after a long absence. As for Furbies, they're still in the
pantheon of hot toys, jabbering in Furbish among themselves.

Source: Schlaifer Nance & Co. 2005

◀ Q U E S T I O N

3   **B) Treason**

According to Dante, the ninth circle of hell is for traitors—
including Judas, Brutus, and Lucifer. Blasphemers reside in
the seventh circle, while unbaptized babies go to the first
circle, *where they get to hang out with noted pagans like
Homer and Socrates.*

Source: Northeastern University Department of English

◀ Q U E S T I O N

Radio Raves—

4 Even for those of you plugged into iPods and earbuds, radio is still a must-have medium. If you stopped a car at random, on almost any street in the country, the odds are the radio would be tuned to which of the following?

A) Country Music
B) Oldies
C) News/Talk

A N S W E R ▶

Joystick Jockeys—

5 A typical game player is most likely to be which of the following?

Myst-ifying!

A) Teenage Boy
B) Adult Woman
C) Your Surgeon

A N S W E R ▶

Gambling Reservations?

6 Casinos on American Indian reservations have been a financial bonanza to the economies of some tribes. What are the chances that a tribe has jumped on this gaming gravy train?

A) 20%
B) 40%
C) 80%

A N S W E R ▶

4   **A) Country Music**

It's not just your hillbilly cousin's "country" any more—even though thinking of George Clooney in *Oh, Brother...* is enough to bring on a lot of gap-toothed smiles. With over 2,000 stations nationwide, country music is still ahead of news/talk's often blood-boiling 1,300 stations and the 800 or so fading oldies.

Source: World Almanac 2005

◀ Q U E S T I O N

5   **B) Adult Woman**

There are more women playing video games than there are teenage boys. (Or maybe they're just better at hiding their addiction.) Research also indicates that laparoscopic surgeons perform better with a solid video gaming history under their belt. So before your ACL reconstruction, buy your doctor a GameBoy. Just make sure she (or he) isn't referring to you as Zelda before the anesthesiologist comes in.

Source: CNN 2004; Psych/IAState

◀ Q U E S T I O N

6   **B) 40%**

So far, only 226 of 567 federally recognized American Indian tribes have going gambling concerns—a bit surprising until you realize where some of the tribes' reservations are sited. But consider Las Vegas and Orlando before Bugsy Siegel and Walt Disney got hold of them—one was a desert, the other a swamp.

Source: FEMA; IndianCountry.com 2005

◀ Q U E S T I O N

Dead Endings—

7 If you had been a victim in one of Agatha Christie's Miss Marple mysteries, you were most likely to have been done in by which of the following?

A) Poisoning
B) Strangling
C) Gunshot

ANSWER ▶

Through Thick or Thin—

8 What are the chances that a book on the bestseller list runs under 400 pages?

No Loss for Words!

A) 20%
B) 40%
C) 60%

ANSWER ▶

Alas, Poor Yorick...

9 When Will Shakespeare sat down to write, what were the odds he'd be working on a comedy rather than a tragedy?

A) About 1 to 2
B) Almost Even Odds
C) Almost 2 to 1

ANSWER ▶

7 ## A) Poisoning

Of the 26 murders Miss Marple solved in her 12 outings in print, there were 9 poisonings, 7 stranglings, 5 gunshot wounds, 1 crushing by rocks (ouch!) and 4 bludgeonings (Oh, those blunt instruments!). If you're traveling in the English countryside, you might want to leave St. Mary Mead off your itinerary.

Source: AgathaChristie.com 2005

◀ Q U E S T I O N

8 ## C) 60%

Although today's bestsellers run the gamut (from Clinton's 1,008-page magnum opus to the featherweight 176-page *He's Just Not That Into You*) most of us are reading "lite." The median length of a top 50 bestseller in 2004 was just 368 pages—just right for a weekend read—unless you're author and critic Harold Bloom, who's been known to devour several of these in one sitting.

Source: U.S. Census Bureau 2004

◀ Q U E S T I O N

9 ## B) Almost Even Odds

Eighteen of the 38 plays attributed to Shakespeare are comedies. If you don't recall anything funny from your high school English class, maybe you were reading one of the 10 tragedies, or the 10 histories. Or maybe you didn't know what you were reading.

Source: Folger Library; Shakespeare.com 2005

◀ Q U E S T I O N

A Real Blockbuster—

10

From 1987 to 2003, an average video store customer was most likely to rent which of the following movies?

A) *Top Gun*
B) *Pretty Woman*
C) *Star Wars*

ANSWER ▶

Dirty Soaps—

11

Among characters on U.S. soap operas, what are the odds that sexual partners are unmarried?

Remotely Familiar?

A) 2 to 1
B) 3 to 1
C) 4 to 1

ANSWER ▶

Triple Crown Player?

12

Only 40 to 50 plays a year ever reach a New York audience. Against odds of about 56 million to 1, which of the following playwrights scored a historical first by winning a Tony, an Oscar, and a Pulitzer?

A) August Wilson
B) Arthur Miller
C) Alfred Uhry

ANSWER ▶

10 **B) *Pretty Woman***

Despite what they might have intended to take home with them, more customers wound up with a hooker for the evening than with either Kelly McGillis (a.k.a. *Charlie*) or Princess Leia. It's the oldest story, really—boy meets working girl, boy gets working girl, boy gets working girl to work only for him. *Star Wars* didn't even make the top ten. Guess the buns don't do it for everyone.

Source: World Almanac *2005*

◀ Q U E S T I O N

11 **B) 3 to 1**

It seems that monogamy on daytime television is as exciting as, well, monogamy in the daytime. This might explain the absence of a home movie section at the local video store and the popularity of the (*wink, wink*) home movie section at the local video store. Whatever sells the most soap wins.

Source: American Academy of Pediatrics

◀ Q U E S T I O N

12 **C) Alfred Uhry**

Stunning achievements for Alfred Uhry who won a Pulitzer Prize for Drama (1988) for his play *Driving Miss Daisy*, an Oscar for Best Screenplay (1989) for the movie version, and a Tony for Best Play for his *Last Night of Ballyhoo* (1997). Both Wilson and Miller have also won the Pulitzer Prize for Drama (Wilson twice) along with numerous other awards.

Source: Tony Archives 2005

◀ Q U E S T I O N

In Like Clint

13 What are the chances that a 1970s Clint Eastwood movie features the actor as a cop or a cowboy?

A) 4 in 15
B) 8 in 15
C) 12 in 15

ANSWER ▶

Which Way Out—

14 Of the following, which is the most likely cause of the premature death of a major rock and roller?

Falling Off the Charts!

A) Plane Crash
B) Traffic Accident
C) Strange Misadventure

ANSWER ▶

No-Show Girls—

15 A woman is least likely to win an Academy Award for which of the following?

A) Cinematography
B) Editing
C) Writing

ANSWER ▶

13   B) 8 in 15

With three turns as Dirty Harry, as well as several other cop and cowpoke roles, Clint spent the '70s looking tough and clutching a major firearm. *(Sort of like Patty Hearst, when you think about it.)* But Eastwood has shown his softer side in films like *Play Misty for Me* and *The Bridges of Madison County* in addition to *Million Dollar Baby*, which earned him Oscars for Best Director and Best Picture of 2004.

Source: IMDB.com

◄ Q U E S T I O N

14   C) Strange Misadventure

Bizarre accidents seem to be the rule among rockers—and not just for Spinal Tap drummers. Among the freak, career-ending occurrences are Chet Baker's defenestration (being thrown out a window), Mama Cass's choking on a ham sandwich (widely reported but not confirmed), and Beach Boy Dennis Wilson's *accidental drowning*.

Source: Fuller Up; The Dead Musicians Directory; Schott's Original Miscellany 2004

◄ Q U E S T I O N

15   A) Cinematography

A woman has never won an Oscar for Best Cinematography, Best Director, or Best Sound. Of course, no woman has ever won for Best Actor or Supporting Actor either, though that one guy from *The Crying Game* came awfully close, as did Hilary Swank in *Boys Don't Cry*. (She won Best Actress, instead.)

Source: Academy of Motion Picture Arts and Sciences

◄ Q U E S T I O N

Here's Johnny—

16

What are the chances that the Jack Nicholson movie you're watching brought Nicholson an Oscar nomination?

A) 10%
B) 30%
C) 40%

ANSWER ▶

No Biz Like Show Biz—

17

An Academy-recognized guild member in which of the following professions stands the best chance of actually winning an Oscar?

A) Musician
B) Writer
C) Actor/Actress

ANSWER ▶

Bat's Entertainment—

18

What was the chance that an actor from the '60s *Batman* TV series would be nominated for an Emmy for playing one of the key villains—the Joker, the Penguin, the Riddler, or Catwoman?

A) Zero
B) 1 in 4
C) 2 in 4

ANSWER ▶

16   B) 30%

Since 1960 Jack Nicholson has been in 40 movies and has been nominated for an Academy Award 12 times. He won for Best Actor in *One Flew Over the Cuckoo's Nest* and *As Good As It Gets*, while nabbing Best Supporting Actor for *Terms of Endearment*. *(Now, he's supposedly up for an ESPY Award based on his supporting role at Lakers games.)*

Source: IMDB.com

◄ Q U E S T I O N

17   A) Musician

If you're a show biz pro, your odds against winning an Oscar are around 11,500 to 1. But the musicians' guilds are not large, and some multiple Oscars are awarded, so musicians stand the best chance, at 1 in 1,667. As for the poor actors, their prospects are about 1 in 20,000. With the humiliating auditions, cutthroat competition, and total lack of job security, one wonders why…*Oh, yes…the fame and fortune.*

Source: Bureau of Labor Statistics

◄ Q U E S T I O N

18   B) 1 in 4

Riddle me this, Batman! In 1966 Frank Gorshin was nominated for an Emmy for Best Supporting Actor in a Comedy as a result of his over-the-top portrayal of the Riddler. And though the *Batman* series now seems campier than summer in the Berkshires, at the time it was credited with saving the venerable comic book franchise from cancellation.

Source: IMDB.com

◄ Q U E S T I O N

Yeah, Yeah, Yeah—

19   What were the chances of a Beatles' Billboard Top 40 hit charting at number one?

A) 24%
B) 38%
C) 74%

ANSWER ▶

Rap It Up

20   As of the end of 2001, a rap album sale was most likely to have been the product of which artist?

Yo Mama!

A) Tupac Shakur
B) MC Hammer
C) Eminem

ANSWER ▶

Laughing Matters—

21   From W. C. Fields to Jim Carrey and Jack Nicholson, Hollywood has turned out a lot of jokers. What's the chance of a comedy being awarded the Oscar for Best Picture?

A) 1 in 5
B) 1 in 10
C) 1 in 20

ANSWER ▶

19 **B) 38%**

Only 20 of the Beatles' 52 Top 40 hits made it to #1—partly because the former Quarrymen became victims of their own success. Some Beatles hits stalled at #2 or #3 because their path to the top was blocked by other Beatles hits. In fact, during one week in 1964, the Beatles simultaneously held the top 5 spots on the chart! *No, "mania" was not too strong a word.*

Source: The Billboard Book of Top 40 Hits, 7th Ed.

◀ Q U E S T I O N

20 **A) Tupac Shakur**

While the *real Slim Shady* was busy standing up, his album sales still couldn't top Tupac's 33.5 million, extraordinarily producing more hits after his death than when he was alive. As for MC, it just wasn't Hammertime.

Source: Guinness Book of World Records 2004

◀ Q U E S T I O N

21 **B) I in I0**

Only 7 comedies have ever won Best Picture. Seven! Can the Academy take themselves that seriously? The *most recent* was *Annie Hall* in '77. The others: *It Happened One Night* ('34), *You Can't Take It with You* ('38), *Going My Way* ('44), *The Apartment* ('60), *Tom Jones* ('63), and *The Sting* ('73). No Marx Brothers! No *Some Like It Hot* or *M*A*S*H* or *As Good As It Gets*. It's no wonder *Woody Allen's* neurotic.

Source: Alexander and Associates/Video Flash

◀ Q U E S T I O N

Funny Little "Focker"?

22 With such memorable roles as *Rain Man* and *Midnight Cowboy*, there's no doubt about Dustin Hoffman's dramatic acting ability. What's the chance that a Hoffman film—selected at random—would be a comedy?

A) 1 in 2
B) 1 in 3
C) 1 in 9

ANSWER ▶

Bald Ambition—

23 What's the likelihood of director Alfred Hitchcock appearing in one of his own films?

One for The Birds!

A) 61%
B) 89%
C) 100%

ANSWER ▶

The Big Draw—

24 While there's a common perception that it takes sex and violence to sell movie tickets, adjusted for inflation, what are the odds that an all-time top-grossing film in the U.S. is animated?

A) 4 in 50
B) 9 in 50
C) 11 in 50

ANSWER ▶

22 **B) 1 in 3**

Mrs. Robinson's boy-toy has been in 37 movies at last count, 12 of which have been comedies—notably *Tootsie*, *The Graduate* (also a drama/romance), and *Wag the Dog*. Not so notably, 1987's *Ishtar*. Although Hoffman's performance in *Meet the Fockers* was considered a standout, the film was not. As almost everybody has said, "Comedy is hard."

Source: IMDB.com

◀ Q U E S T I O N

23 **C) 100%**

That's right. The Master of Suspense was also the Master of I'm-Going-to-Be-in-Every-One-of-My-41- Pictures. He usually made his appearance just when you'd stopped looking for him. But how, you may wonder, did he find his way into *Lifeboat*, a movie which featured 10 actors and no extras? Hitchcock's before and after photos were on the back of a prop newspaper, in an ad for "Reduco Obesity Slayer."

Source: http://hitchcock.tv/cam/cameos.html

◀ Q U E S T I O N

24 **B) 9 in 50**

Animated films pop up with surprising frequency on the top-50 films list. Disney set the stage with recyclable classics like *The Jungle Book* (#9), *Snow White* (#10), *101 Dalmatians* (#12), and more recently, *The Lion King* (#26). So far, the only non-Disney animation in the all-time top 50 is *Shrek* (#27) from DreamWorks. And now we even have animated porno flicks. *What would Walt say?*

Source: MovieTimes.com 2005

◀ Q U E S T I O N

Get 'em All?
Take a Bow!

10

Sports:
Feats
&
Defeats

"Life's too short for chess."
— H.J. BYRON —

Ever wonder how cold the waters of the English Channel are...or the odds of swimming it to France?

How about making it to the pros...or completing an unassisted triple play?

Could a gelding beat the field at the Kentucky Derby?

In sports feats and defeats—it's all about winning and losing. Are you game?

Dover Souls—

1

Maybe it's the climate, but it seems those crazy Brits will do just about anything to invade France. What's the chance of making a successful 21-mile Channel swim from England to France?

A) 1 in 5
B) 2 in 5
C) 3 in 5

ANSWER ▶

The Vision Thing—

2

Based on participant percentages, in which of the following sports are you most likely to suffer an eye injury?

Focus on the Question!

A) Badminton
B) Baseball
C) Boxing

ANSWER ▶

A Kick in the Grass—

3

If you were to pick the soccer team most likely to go to the finals of the World Cup and win it, you'd choose which one of the following?

A) Brazil
B) Argentina
C) Italy

ANSWER ▶

1   B) 2 in 5

About 40% of those attempting to swim the 60°F English Channel from Dover, England, to Calais, France, actually go all the way. The record for the swim is Allison Streeter's 9 hours and 30 minutes in 1996. The small army of successful swimmers (2 to 1, men to women) now numbers about 600, who, if placed end to end, would look like 600 people turning blue, end to end.

Source: Channel Swimming Association 2003

◄ QUESTION

2   A) Badminton

Everyone's favorite backyard pastime is actually the #1 most dangerous sport in terms of eye injuries. Maybe no one's paying attention because they're all too busy giggling at the word "shuttlecock."

Source: CDC; NCHS 2004

◄ QUESTION

3   A) Brazil

Those boys from Brazil have closed the deal, so to speak, with five wins in seven tries. Italy's won half of its six visits to the finals, and Argentina has won half of its four tries. By all accounts there was a simple reason for the difference in how the teams performed. It's spelled P-E-L-É, still the greatest player in the history of the game.

Source: University of Toronto 2003

◄ QUESTION

Making It in the Pros—

4   Making those big bucks as a pro athlete is the dream of millions of high school kids. The odds are 10,000 to 1 *against* a male athlete in the U.S. making it to the pros in which of the following sports?

A) Wrestling
B) Football
C) Basketball

ANSWER ▶

Royalty-Fed Football—

5   Forget wins and national championships, which of the following schools would you bet on to lead the nation in that all-important spectator sport—*merchandising?*

A) Michigan
B) Georgia
C) Oklahoma

ANSWER ▶

Losing and Winning?

6   For a player on a losing team, the odds of getting the MVP award for a championship game or series is most likely in which of the following competitions?

A) NBA Championships
B) NFL Super Bowl
C) NHL Stanley Cup

ANSWER ▶

4 ## C) Basketball

While football players barely have a prayer with odds at 6,000 to 1 against them, landing a spot on those five-man basketball teams is even more unlikely. And most high school wrestling does nothing to prepare you for the "pros"— unless you're in one of those body-slamming charter schools sanctioned by WWF.

Source: NCAA

◀ Q U E S T I O N

5 ## A) Michigan

Go Wolverines! Even though you haven't won a national championship—or even a top-five ranking in recent memory—you've won *where it really counts,* in the wallets. Georgia has risen to a bulldogged 3rd. And the Oklahoma Sooners, a perennial national football power, is 4th. Fortunately, there's still more than enough revenue from TV and game attendance to get them all through their goals.

Source: College Licensing Corporation 2005

◀ Q U E S T I O N

6 ## C) NHL Stanley Cup

Hockey seems more attuned to the nobility of defeat, awarding five MVPs to losers, compared to just one each for the NBA and the NFL over similar time periods. And there's nothing like an MVP award to get a big toothless grin out of one of those hockey puckers.

Source: ESPN Sports Almanac 2003

◀ Q U E S T I O N

An Investment in Bonds—

7
During Barry Bonds's record-setting 2001 season, what were the chances that the slugger would hit a home run in the Giants' own, Pac Bell Park?

A) 26%
B) 36%
C) 46%

ANSWER ▶

Perfect Plays—

8
From the first MLB World Series in 1903 through the 2002 series, which of the following is the least likely play?

Who's on Third?

A) Pitching a Perfect Game
B) Unassisted Triple Play
C) "Who Let the Dogs Out?"

ANSWER ▶

Home Runs?

9
Rickey Henderson holds the all-time stolen base record with around 1,300 steals. What are the odds of Henderson's stealing home compared to that of the late Ty Cobb?

A) 6 to 1
B) 2 to 1
C) 1 to 6

ANSWER ▶

7   **C) 46%**

In 2001 Bonds homered 37 times at Pac Bell Park. Of course, if you just liked watching the smooth grace of his striding to first base, you also could watch him walk at least once in every four plate appearances!

Source: ESPN 2003

◀ Q U E S T I O N

8   **B) Unassisted Triple Play**

There have been only 12 unassisted triple plays compared to 16 perfect games in the history of Major League Baseball. Computing the playing of "Who Let the Dogs Out?" exceeds all existing computer capacities.

Source: Seattle Post-Intelligencer *2003*

◀ Q U E S T I O N

9   **C) 1 to 6**

Cobb's cleat-first run-and-lunge style terrorized opponents and got him the all-time record for stealing home with 26 runs compared to only 4 for the otherwise far more prodigious base swiper, Henderson. In addition, Ty Cobb still holds the record for double steals at 22 and triple steals at 6. But there's *no record* of Cobb ever being called "a nice guy."

Source: Baseball's Most Fabulous Feats *2005*

◀ Q U E S T I O N

Balls to the Walls—

10   Four home runs for one player in a single game is tops, so far, for players in both leagues. What are the odds of a National League player having 4 four-baggers in a game, compared to that of an American Leaguer?

A) 5 to 1
B) 3 to 1
C) 2 to 1

ANSWER ▶

Heavy Lifting?

11   Back in pre-steroid days, baseball's big hitters swung bats that weighed in at up to 48 ounces. Odds are today's miraculously muscular player's "lumber" averages which of the following?

A) 52 ounces
B) 48 ounces
C) 36 ounces

ANSWER ▶

Perfect Pitch—

12   For every batter dreaming of a home run on every swing, there's a pitcher praying that every pitch is a strike—retiring the side in a sweet nine pitches. What are the odds the NL pitchers have done this compared to the AL?

A) 1 to 1
B) 2 to 1
C) 3 to 1

ANSWER ▶

10 **C) 2 to 1**

Although the American League has had some heavy hitters like Babe Ruth, Mickey Mantle, Lou Gehrig, and Rocky Colavito, 10 of the 15 batters with 4 home runs in a game were in the National League, including Willie Mays, Mike Schmidt, Bob Horner, and, most recently, Shawn Green. While we're counting, we have to wonder how many different opposing pitchers these guys faced on their four-ball-blasts.

Source: Baseball's Most Fabulous Feats 2005

◀ Q U E S T I O N

11 **C) 36 ounces**

As many a men's magazine has reassured its readers, it's not the size that matters! And some would claim there's more bounce to the ounce because of the balls, not just juiced-up batters. The aerodynamics of being able to swing faster goes along with "enhanced" performance to make those balls fly farther—though the "shrunken nuts" side effect of steroids seems like a big sacrifice—*even* for baseball.

Source: MLB 2005

◀ Q U E S T I O N

12 **B) 2 to 1**

The NL has clear superiority here with the likes of Sandy Koufax pitching two three-for-threes, joined by Bruce Sutter, Randy Johnson, and a host of others. A little over a third of these remarkable innings belong to the AL—including the expected throwers like Lefty Grove (twice), Nolan Ryan, Ron Guidry, and Pedro Martinez. Since the umpires only have to count to three on one hand, *it's good for them, too.*

Source: Baseball-Reference.com 2005

◀ Q U E S T I O N

Free and Easy—

13   Mark Price holds the NBA record for the highest career-free-throw percentage. What were the chances he'd make the shot?

A) 8.5 of 10
B) 9.0 of 10
C) 9.5 of 10

ANSWER ▶

Peter Piper Picked a Peck—

14   A Top Ten NBA draft pick in 2002 was most likely to have just come from which of the following?

A Long Shot!

A) High School
B) A Foreign Country
C) Jail

ANSWER ▶

Helping Hands—

15   In basketball, your scoring usually goes way up if your teammates get you the ball. Which of the following players would be most likely to give you an assist?

A) Magic Johnson
B) John Stockton
C) Bob Cousy

ANSWER ▶

13 **B) 9.0 of 10**

Price sunk 2,135 free throws in his pro career at a .904 clip. Pretty impressive, until you consider that at age 61, retired dairy farmer Ted St. Martin hit *5,221* free throws in a row. Wow! There's a lesson here, we're just not sure what it is.

Source: NCAA 2003; sharpshooterfreethrows.com

◀ Q U E S T I O N

14 **B) Foreign Country**

Led by former Shanghai Shark Yao Ming, three of 2002's top ten came from abroad, compared to two from Duke University and one, Amare Stoudemire, from high school. *Jail, on the other hand, is usually reserved for one's first NBA off-season.*

Source: NBA 2003

◀ Q U E S T I O N

15 **A) Magic Johnson**

In basketball as in life, it helps to be in the right place at the right time. Johnson earned his nickname "Magic" as much for his passing ability (12.4 assists) as for his wizardry at shooting. Stockton ranks second all-time with 10.4 and Cousy, the guy who seemed to have invented the stellar pass and cool ball handling, ranks sixth with 8.6 per game. *Not bad for two white guys.*

Source: NBA 2004

◀ Q U E S T I O N

Passing Grade—

16

Dan Marino needs no introduction to football fans in terms of his all-around passing ability. What's the chance of one of his passes connecting for a touchdown?

A) 1 in 21
B) 1 in 15
C) 1 in 9

ANSWER ▶

National Champions?

17

Between 1940 and 1998, which NCAA Division I team was most likely to have won a national football championship?

Don't Rush Me, Now!

A) Notre Dame
B) Alabama
C) Oklahoma

ANSWER ▶

Always a Great Reception—

18

When it comes to pass receivers, there's San Francisco 49er Jerry Rice—and everybody else. What are the chances of Rice's carrying a completed pass for a touchdown during the course of his incredible career?

A) 5%
B) 10%
C) 15%

ANSWER ▶

16 **C) 1 in 9**

Marino's is an amazing saga of a low draft pick going on to become Rookie of the Year for the Miami Dolphins, and then setting all-time league records for most yards passing (58,913 yards), most yards passing per game (helps to get to that first number), most touchdown passes, and, while not listed in any NFL books, a sure front-of-the-liner anytime at Joe's Stone Crab or pretty much any other line in Miami.

Source: AJC 2005

◀ Q U E S T I O N

17 **A) Notre Dame**

The Fighting Irish have won nine times, compared to seven victories for Alabama's Crimson Tide and six for the Oklahoma Sooners. Those of you trying to figure out why we didn't list Harvard and Yale just didn't pick up on the fact that this was football and not the national pastime of Latvia—*chess.*

Source: AJC 2005

◀ Q U E S T I O N

18 **C) 15%**

In addition to getting first downs with a record-setting 14.5 yards per carry, Rice (#80)—on average— scored a TD better than 1 in every 7 times that he caught the ball. Could he have done any better with Dan Marino passing to him—or vice versa? *Naaah. That would be too piggy to even consider.*

Source: AJC 2005

◀ Q U E S T I O N

Master Blasters—

19   If you were to bet on any one of Jack Nicklaus's winning scores in the Masters Tournament against the winning scores of Tiger Woods's four victories, what's the chance that any of Jack's would beat Tiger's?

A) 1 Out of 12
B) 1 Out of 8
C) 1 Out of 4

A N S W E R ▶

Dead at 17

20   Reaching the short green in the center of the lake on number seventeen of the Tournament Players Club at Sawgrass is just a wedge for most pros. In championship play, odds are that how many balls will end up in the water?

A) 15
B) 30
C) 60

A N S W E R ▶

Heaven Sent—

21   Birdies abound in pro golf tournaments the way bogeys do in the amateur ranks— almost routinely. For a *pro*, which of the following is most likely to be a 1 in 6,500 long shot?

A) Hole in One
B) Double Eagle
C) Lightning Strike

A N S W E R ▶

19 **B) I Out of 8**

This won't please the ardent Nicklaus fans, but only I of Jack's 6 wins (his 271 in '65), would have beaten Tiger's last 3—but not his record-setting 270 win in '97. In fact, Tiger has averaged about 5 strokes better in his 4 wins (273) than Jack has in his 6 (278). So if you still want to bet in a battle between a Tiger and a Bear, *we'd recommend going for the Woods.*

Source: PGA 2005

◀ Q U E S T I O N

20 **B) 30**

While there have been 6 holes in one over the 23 years of the Sawgrass TPC tournament, the gut-wrenching experience of seeing a lead—or chance of making the cut—vanish underwater is an oft-repeated experience: nearly 30 times a tournament and about *150,000* times a year in regular play. In 2002 under windy conditions, even the pros' normal 30 shot up to 75. *Hey, that's golf!*

Source: AJC 2005

◀ Q U E S T I O N

21 **A) Hole in One**

The pros ace in I in 6,500. By comparison, a double eagle is estimated at I in 6 million—the rarest in golf—in part, because most players can't reach a par-5 green in just 2 shots. A lightning strike, normally I in 550,000, could be almost a sure thing if you're one of those "tough" guys who continue running around the course with metal sticks in their hands during a thunderstorm!

Source: PGA 2005

◀ Q U E S T I O N

Call the Fall—

22   There's never been a fighter with the size, speed, and creative style of Muhammad Ali—nor another with the ability to call the round of an opponent's fall. In which round of a fight was Ali most likely to deliver a KO?

A) Round Five
B) Round Seven
C) Round Twelve

ANSWER ▶

Hit Men—

23   For most pugilists, the fine art of boxing comes down to knocking out an opponent—before the opponent gets to them. Which of the following sluggers was most likely to KO his opponents?

A) Joe Louis
B) Jack Dempsey
C) Rocky Marciano

ANSWER ▶

Pocket Change—

24   Pocket billiards, or pool, is all about putting the ball in a designated pocket—until you don't. And Willie Mosconi was pool's greatest. What were the odds of Mosconi's winning a World Championship match?

A) 15 to 1
B) 10 to 1
C) 5 to 1

ANSWER ▶

22   **B) Round Seven**

In 61 fights, Ali KO'd 37 opponents in the seventh round. He only got 3 in the fifth and 4 in the twelfth. Except for a few contests—like the14-round "Thrilla in Manila" and the 8-round dismantling of George Foreman in Zaire— less than half made it past the seventh round.

Source: The World Health Report, WHO 2004; CDC 2004

◄ Q U E S T I O N

23   **C) Rocky Marciano**

The Massachusetts Mauler not only retired undefeated, he put out the lights on 43 of 49 opponents. Dempsey, another brawler, took out 50 of the 60 guys he fought. While Joe Louis's KO record wasn't quite that of Marciano's and Dempsey's, the Bronx Bomber was a lethal fighter and demonstrated it dramatically when he demolished Max Schmeling in the first round of their rematch in 1938.

Source: Provident Medical Institute, 2001; AAFP 1998

◄ Q U E S T I O N

24   **A) 15 to 1**

In 16 tournaments Mosconi lost only one—a level of accomplishment unmatched in the history of pool. The elegant Mr. Mosconi also established the still-unbroken record of putting in 526 balls in a row, *without a miss.* If you're wondering where Minnesota Fats was during Mosconi's reign, you'd probably have found him looking for someone to hustle…or something to eat.

Source: World Billiard Congress 2005

◄ Q U E S T I O N

For the Smell of the Roses—

25 A Kentucky Derby winner (usually a stallion or a mare) means cash at the gate and even more in breeding fees. What are the chances of the Derby winner being a gelding with nothing to go for but the gate?

A) 2 in 130
B) 6 in 130
C) 12 in 130

ANSWER ▶

For Love or Money?

26 Of the following tennis greats, which one had the best odds of winning Wimbledon during the best ten years of his career?

The Grass Is Greener...

A) John McEnroe
B) Björn Borg
C) Pete Sampras

ANSWER ▶

Against the Clock—

27 The action—and accidents—in NASCAR racing can be heart-stopping for the fans. But of all the drivers and crews during 1990–2000 seasons what was the chance that a participant's death was caused by heart attack?

A) 1 in 8
B) 1 in 96
C) 1 in 260

ANSWER ▶

25 **B) 6 in 130**

With the promise of little more than the crack of the crop and carrots and oats at the end of the race, 6 of the Derby winners have been geldings—the most recent being Funny Cide in 2003.

Source: Thoroughbred Times *2005*

◄ Q U E S T I O N

26 **C) Pete Sampras**

Borg was close behind with five wins in a row between '76 and '80, when he retired. But Sampras was practically unstoppable, winning 7 of 10 championship matches between '93 and 2002. McEnroe, entertaining on and off the court, screamed his way to two victories in '83 and '84 and amazingly scored three doubles victories with Peter Fleming in '79, '83, and '84.

Source: Wimbledon.com *2005*

◄ Q U E S T I O N

27 **A) 1 in 8**

Maybe it's the tension of moving at over 200 mph with a bunch of crazy people chasing you...Or maybe it's the fast food and tobacco, but between 1990 and 2001, there were 260 racing deaths, 32 from heart attacks. As in business, so go sports—*lead, follow, or get out of the way!*

Source: USA Today *2001*

◄ Q U E S T I O N

Ping or Pong?

28 What are the chances that the winner of an Olympic gold medal in table tennis will be Chinese?

A) 78%
B) 55%
C) 34%

ANSWER ▶

Watch Where You Put Those Hands—

29 What is the chance that a U.S. high school wrestler is a girl?

Is That a Half Nelson?

A) 1 in 75
B) 1 in 750
C) 1 in 7,500

ANSWER ▶

The Power Behind the Thrown—

30 Which of the following objects is most likely to have been thrown more than 80 meters in men's Olympic competition?

A) A Discus
B) A Hammer
C) A Dwarf

ANSWER ▶

28 **A) 78%**

Of the 18 players who have won Olympic gold in singles or doubles table tennis, 14 are Chinese, 3 are Korean, and 1 is Jan-Ove Waldner of Sweden. Why, do you suppose, are those Chinese athletes so adept at paddling their little white balls?

Source: About.com

◄ Q U E S T I O N

29 **A) 1 in 75**

Of the nearly 250,000 high school wrestlers in the U.S. in 2002, just over 3,400 were female. But if you ask some coaches, they're *all* girls.

Source: USA Wrestling

◄ Q U E S T I O N

30 **B) A Hammer**

Believe it or not, hammer throwers regularly outdistance both shot putters and discus throwers. Dwarf tossing has never been a sanctioned Olympic event.

Source: Encyclopedia Britannica Almanac 2003

◄ Q U E S T I O N